RECONCILIATION

Catholic Spirituality for Adults

General Editor
Michael Leach

Other Books in the Series
Prayer

RECONCILIATION

❋

Robert F. Morneau

Maryknoll, New York 10545

Founded in 1970, Orbis Books endeavors to publish works that enlighten the mind, nourish the spirit, and challenge the conscience. The publishing arm of the Maryknoll Fathers and Brothers, Orbis seeks to explore the global dimensions of the Christian faith and mission, to invite dialogue with diverse cultures and religious traditions, and to serve the cause of reconciliation and peace. The books published reflect the views of their authors and do not represent the official position of the Maryknoll Society. To learn more about Maryknoll and Orbis Books, please visit our website at www.maryknoll.org.

Library of Congress Cataloging-in-Publication Data

Morneau, Robert F., 1938-
    Reconciliation / Robert F. Morneau.
        p.   cm. – (Christ Jesus, the way)
    ISBN 978-1-57075-713-6
    1. Penance. 2. Reconciliation – Religious aspects – Catholic Church.
  3. Forgiveness. 4. Mercy. I. Title.
  BX2260.M67 2007
  234'.166 – dc22

                                                                        2007005779

Dedicated to
Most Reverend Aloysius J. Wycislo
Friend, Mentor, Bishop
(1908–2005)

The author would like to acknowledge the editorial help of Tony and Jackie Staley.

Contents

Introduction to Catholic Spirituality for Adults

CATHOLIC SPIRITUALITY FOR ADULTS explores the deepest dimension of spirituality, that place in the soul where faith meets understanding. When we reach that place we begin to see as if for the first time. We are like the blind man in the Gospel who could not believe his eyes: "And now I see!"

Catholicism is about seeing the good of God that is in front of our eyes, within us, and all around us. It is about learning to see Christ Jesus with the eyes of Christ Jesus, the Way, the Truth, and the Life.

Only when we *see* who we are as brothers and sisters of Christ and children of God can we begin to *be* like Jesus and walk in his Way. "As you think in your heart, so you are" (Prov. 23:7).

Catholic Spirituality for Adults is for those of us who want to make real, here and now, the words we too once learned. It is designed to help us go beyond information to transformation. "When I was a child; I spoke as a child, I understood as a child, I thought as a child; but when I became an adult, I put away childish things" (1 Cor. 13:11).

The contributors to the series are the best Catholic authors writing today. We have asked them to explore the deepest dimension of their own faith and to share with us what they are learning to see. Topics covered range from prayer — "Be still and know that I am God" (Ps. 46:10) — to our purpose in life — coming to know "that God has given us eternal life, and that this life is in his Son" (1 John 5:11) — to simply getting through the day — "Put on compassion, kindness, humility, and love" (Col. 3:12).

Each book in this series reflects Christ's active and loving presence in the world. The authors celebrate our membership in the mystical body of Christ, help us to understand our spiritual unity with the entire family of God, and encourage us to express Christ's mission of love, peace, and reconciliation in our daily lives.

Catholic Spirituality for Adults is the fruit of a publishing partnership between Orbis Books, the publishing arm of the Catholic Foreign Mission Society of America (Maryknoll), and RCL Benziger, a leading provider of religious and family life education for all ages. This series is rooted in vital Catholic traditions and committed to a continuing standard of excellence.

Michael Leach
General Editor

Author's Introduction

W E LIVE IN AN ERA of self-improvement. We find it in a large section of the bookstore, in numerous advice columns in newspapers and magazines, and in TV shows. Then there are the exercise videos to improve the body and the how-to TV shows to improve the home. Psychologists and counselors also thrive.

Despite all our efforts, we still know, or at least sense, that something is missing. We cannot tame the innate restlessness within. St. Augustine of Hippo said it best: "Our hearts are restless, Lord, until they rest in you."

That's where spiritual direction and confession come in. Through them we can find the interior resources — the grace of God — to bring about the changes we want in life. Through confession we can learn to deal with the disorders within us and to experience the healing power of God's love through the forgiveness of our sins.

There is an old Latin adage that contains a wealth of wisdom: *In omnibus respice finem,* "In all things look to the end."

In seeking to understand the sacrament of reconciliation we can do no better than begin with the goal and aim of the sacrament: union and unity. We creatures are made for oneness with God and oneness with each other. This Christian life is all about union and unity. So, too, regarding the mission and nature of the church. In Vatican II's document on the church, *Lumen Gentium,* we are given with great clarity what the church is about:

> Christ is the Light of nations. Because this is so, this Sacred Synod gathered together in the Holy Spirit eagerly desires, by proclaiming the Gospel to every creature, to bring the light of Christ to all men, a light brightly visible on the countenance of the Church. Since the Church is in Christ like a sacrament or as a sign and instrument both of a very closely knit union with God and of the unity of the whole human race, it desires now to unfold more fully to the faithful of the Church and to the whole world its own inner nature and universal mission.[1]

But something has gone wrong. God's plan for union and unity has been thwarted. Something has injured, even broken, the oneness that Jesus prayed for so intensely in St. John's Gospel. That something is sin, attitudes and acts that rupture our relationship with God, with others, with our self, and with creation.

And God's response to this disobedience of his creatures? God, the God who is Love, expresses that divine affection through mercy and forgiveness. God sent his Son, Incarnate Love and Mercy, into the world to reconcile us to the Father. Jesus came to bring us peace, the gift of the Holy Spirit. Through the mystery of the cross, our redemption, union and unity are once again possible. And in that reconciliation we come to know God's peace and joy.

Just as we have been forgiven and restored to a life of grace, we in turn are sent forth to be peacemakers. We are to reconcile, as agents of God's plan for union and unity. Our mission and ministry is one with that of Jesus and the church: to restore all things in Christ.

It is within this framework that we might prayerfully reflect on the sacrament of reconciliation. Since our concept of God is vital to our understanding of the sacraments, the first chapter will describe various images of God that come from the Scriptures and our rich tradition. Then we must deal with who we are as human beings. A basic anthropology or understanding of the human person is necessary if we are to get the sacrament of reconciliation "right." Chapter 3 presents the context for reconciliation, while chapter 4 addresses the mysteries of grace and sin. What is this life of Christ within us and what does sin do to diminish that life? Chapter 5 offers ten principles of reconciliation; chapter 6 deals with reconciliation from a sacramental point of view. The last two chapters are more pastoral and literary. Chapter 7 articulates questions that people often raise regarding the sacrament. The final chapter offers a poetic perspective by using metaphors and images that engage the imagination as we celebrate God's forgiveness and mercy.

Our God is a faithful God. The divine promise of presence assures us that God does not abandon us when, through sin, we turn away from God's love. The sacrament of reconciliation in the end is a sacrament of peace and joy.

The Mystery of God's Mercy

THE MOST RECENT doctor of the church, St. Thérèse of Lisieux (1873–97), used two words to describe her understanding of God: "Love" and "Mercy"! We do well to listen to the wisdom figures of our Christian tradition; we do well to listen to the mystics who have experienced God firsthand.

If words such as "love" and "mercy" sometimes fail us in our attempt to understand and appropriate the mysteries of our faith, we can turn to the artists who give us a visual representation of our more abstract theological language. When we speak of God as a God of mercy, we can do no better than to gaze prayerfully on a work of Rembrandt Harmenszoon van Rijn, one of Europe's greatest artists. His popular and powerful *The Return of the Prodigal Son* captures in exquisite detail the mercy of our gracious God. The father embraces the prodigal son with infinite tenderness. We know the rest of the story as found in Luke 15:11–32 — the father pleading with the elder, "good" son to extend to his wayward brother the same mercy that resides in the father's heart.

This portrait, indeed this graced parable, attempts to convince all of us that God's mercy is available to all. But we need to put ourselves in the way of this gift by returning home. We can decide to remain afar. Or, even worse, we can decide to be at home in God's presence with a judgmental attitude that refuses to share with others the mercy and love the Father gives us daily. Spending several hours contemplating Rembrandt's painting can bring about a deep conversion of heart. In 1994, Henri Nouwen's *The Return of the Prodigal Son: A Story of Homecoming* was published. It offers a rich, prayerful analysis of Rembrandt's work. It drives home the point that all of us, in the various circumstances of our lives, are all the characters in the painting: the frail, merciful father; the sinful prodigal; the angry elder one; the bystanders observing God's mercy from afar.

Just as a doctor of the church (Thérèse of Lisieux) and a painter (Rembrandt) express their notion of a merciful God in words and art, so too does the poet Jessica Powers (1905–88). Known in religious life as Sr. Miriam of the Holy Spirit, Jessica Powers used her gift of poetic language to communicate her experiences of our Triune God. In "The Mercy of God" we are given a haunting description of how a soul moves from fear to liberation by the grace of God. This poem is worthy of serious prayer:

The Mercy of God

I am copying down in a book from my heart's
      archives
the day that I ceased to fear God with a shadowy
      fear.
Would you name it the day I measured my
      column of virtue
and sighted through windows of merit a crown
      that was near?
Ah, no, it was rather the day I began to see truly
that I came forth from nothing and ever toward
      nothingness tend,

that the works of my hands are foolishness
        wrought in the presence
of the worthiest king in a kingdom that never
        shall end.
I rose up from the acres of self that I tended
        with passion
and defended with flurries of pride;
I walked out of myself and went into the woods
        of God's mercy,
and here I abide.
There is greenness and calmness and coolness, a
        soft leafy covering
from the judgment of sun overhead,
and the hush of His peace, and the moss of His
        mercy to tread.
I have naught but my will seeking God; even
        love burning in me
is a fragment of infinite loving and never my
        own.
And I fear God no more; I go forward to wander
        forever
in a wilderness made of His infinite mercy
        alone.[1]

                              — Jessica Powers

In this verse we witness the poet's movement from self to
God. In confessional honesty, the poet tells of her fear, of
an awareness of her nothingness, of her foolishness and passion and pride, of her need to transcend "the acres of self."
And what is the new world and life she now enjoys? It is
the experience of God's infinite mercy that brings peace and
greenness and calmness and coolness. The grace given is that

of seeking but one thing: God's will. Once we make that commitment, fear vanishes and God's wilderness of mercy becomes our home.

It is in the sacrament of reconciliation that we too can experience various aspects of God's mercy. When we name and take responsibility for those attitudes and behaviors that separate us from God and our sisters and brothers, we become disposed to the influx of God's forgiveness. However, when we fudge and dally and procrastinate in dealing with the dark side of our lives, the offered grace has little effect on our spiritual well-being. We can be assured, however, of God's fidelity, and that God's forgiveness is always available to us through the sacrament of reconciliation.

The Quality of Mercy

St. Bernard wrote: "The prophet does not exempt himself from the general wretchedness, lest he be left out of the mercy too." "Wretchedness" is a strong term. In fact, one can turn to our contemporary hymnals and find that an optional text — "That saved and set me free" — is offered to replace the traditional line ("That saved a wretch like me") in "Amazing Grace." But there is a corollary here that is frightening. If we are not in touch with our wretchedness, of that dimension of our human condition that alienates us from God's presence, then we fail to recognize our need for God's mercy. To deny that we need God's mercy is to say that we do not need Jesus because he said, "It is not the healthy that need a doctor, but the sick; I have not come to invite virtuous people, but to call sinners to repentance" (Luke 5:31–32). One of Flannery O'Connor's characters faced this dilemma:

"Mr. Head had never known before what mercy felt like because he had been too good to deserve any, but he felt he knew now."

But just the briefest reflection, both in regard to our personal lives and our collective existence, gives major evidence that we all need divine mercy. We hurt each other in many ways: sharp words, lack of affirmation, broken promises, cruelty, neglect, abuse — the list is endless. And as a community, be it nation or family or parish or organization, we have policies and behaviors that injure others. We do need grace, the grace of mercy, to deal with the general wretchedness of existence.

When we name and take responsibility for those attitudes and behaviors that separate us from God and our sisters and brothers, we become disposed to the influx of God's forgiveness.

Pope John Paul II wrote an encyclical letter, *Dives in Misericordia,* in November of 1980. In the last section of that letter he offers this reflection on the richness of God's mercy:

The Church proclaims the truth of God's mercy revealed in the crucified and risen Christ, and she professes it in various ways. Furthermore, she seeks to practice mercy towards people through people, and she sees in this an indispensable condition for solicitude for a better and "more human" world, today and tomorrow. However, at no time and in no historical period — especially at a moment as critical as our own — can the Church forget the prayer that is a cry for the mercy of God amid the many forms of evil which weigh upon humanity and threaten it. Precisely this is the fundamental right and duty of the Church in Christ Jesus, her right and duty towards God and towards humanity. The more the human conscience succumbs to secularization, loses its sense of the very meaning of the word "mercy," moves away from God and distances itself from the mystery of mercy, the more the Church has the right and the duty to appeal to the God of mercy "with loud cries." These "loud cries" should be the mark of the Church of our times, cries uttered to God to implore His mercy, the certain manifestation of which she professes and proclaims as having already come in Jesus crucified and risen, that is, in the Paschal Mystery. It is this mystery which bears within itself the most complete revelation of mercy, that is, of that love which is more powerful than death, more powerful than sin and every evil, the love which lifts man up when he falls into the abyss and frees him from the greatest threats.[2]

Pope John Paul II was a realist. Having lived through World War II as a youth and having a deep grasp of the forces of good and evil in the twentieth century, he was keenly aware of our need for God's mercy as revealed in Jesus. For the pope, sin was the force that diminishes life and disrupts community. His plea that we respect human dignity became his battle cry. But just as important was the need for forgiveness, for the grace of God's mercy so needed to transform both the human heart and human society. John Paul II, a man of deep faith, knew the price that Christ paid for our salvation — the very giving of his life on the cross.

In Shakespeare's *The Merchant of Venice,* Portia cries out:

> The quality of mercy is not strain'd.
> It droppeth as the gentle rain from heaven
> Upon the place beneath.
> It is twice blest:
> It blesseth him that gives and him that takes.
> (Act IV, sc. 1, ll. 182–85)

Maybe the metaphor from nature captures the essence of God's mercy: the gentle rain that falls from heaven. And that rain falls on all, without discrimination. Our task is to receive God's grace and then, once received, pass it on to others.

A story about God's mercy might help to highlight the centrality of divine forgiveness. Two people got into a theological argument about the attributes of God. One person claimed that truth was the greatest attribute; the other argued that it was beauty. A third individual, hearing the heated conversation, proposed: "In the end, all we have is the mercy of God. This is the greatest of the divine attributes." Whatever the case, we know that the God revealed in Jesus is a God of truth, goodness, and mercy. And maybe all of these qualities are simply different ways of saying that God is Love.

God's Word

Put away from you all bitterness and wrath and anger and wrangling and slander, together with all malice, and be kind to one another, tenderhearted, forgiving one another, as God in Christ has forgiven you. (Eph. 4:32)

Blessed are the merciful, for they shall receive mercy.

(Matt. 5:7)

"Go and learn what this means, 'I desire mercy, not sacrifice.' For I have come to call not the righteous but sinners." (Matt. 9:13)

Should you not have had mercy on your fellow slave, as I had mercy on you? (Matt. 18:33)

In reflecting upon the grace of mercy, we must begin at the proper starting point: God's mercy given to us. Here is God's love in the face of our guilt and shame. There are situations so horrendous that it is impossible for us to forgive others and be merciful without the power of the Holy Spirit. It is Jesus in us who extends divine mercy to others. That mercy is to flow through our words and attitudes because of the empowerment of the Holy Spirit.

Brutal honesty is required here. All of us, without exception, have sinned; all of us need God's forgiveness and mercy. St. Paul constantly reminded his people (as well as himself) that "God in Christ has forgiven us." To withhold this mercy from our fellow sinners is to deny discipleship. As followers of Jesus, we are to continue his mission and ministry. As agents of reconciliation, we bring healing to the world through the power of grace.

Conclusion

Poets have the marvelous ability to use metaphors to describe deep theological realities. In her poem "Retreat Magnificat, 1990," Sr. Anne Higgins, D.C., speaks of God's mercy as having the cleansing power of rain. She does this by paraphrasing the great canticle of Mary in her visitation to Elizabeth (Luke 1:46–55).

Retreat Magnificat, 1990

My heart shudders in God's close breath,
and I stand silent before majesty and mercy.
For God has fluted his care for me
through the song of the Wood Thrush.
God shines in the eyes of those who love me,
startles me with unending surprises.

God's mercy rains on me.
I lift my face to drink
its cleansing power.

God's humor overturns my selfish plans,
shakes out my choking impatience.
God favors me with friends;
graces me with poetry
and intuition.
And I praise God with these,
with the gift of myself.

God upholds the promise
lived through Jesus
present in our world,
and in my heart.[3]

Chapter Two _____

The Mystery of the Human Person

PHILOSOPHERS, theologians, psychologists, and sociologists have struggled from the beginning of time to describe, much less define, the essence of a human person. The enigma of the human personality cannot be captured in words or symbols. Yet we do have some degree of self-knowledge, and it is important that we strive for self-understanding and self-acceptance. More, it is important that once we know, understand, and accept ourselves, that we transcend our limited lives by reaching out to others.

From a theological point of view, the human person is a beloved creature. God creates and sustains all of life; God loves humanity and has endowed it with the richest of blessings: intelligence, freedom, desires. It is because we can reject our creaturehood and fail to believe that we are loved that we need reconciliation. We sin by devaluing ourselves and others; we sin by attempting to live an autonomous life, separated from God and the human community.

From a poetic point of view (à la Gerard Manley Hopkins), the human person is an "immortal diamond." There is a preciousness and dignity about every person that demands our respect and reverence. Though at times diamonds-in-the-rough, we retain a splendor that nothing can take away. And just as diamonds are "forever," the human person is immortal, destined for eternal life. We have here mystery upon mystery. But within the context of the mysterious nature of the human person is the reality of sin. Sin refuses to appreciate and honor the value and sacredness of every person, of every "immortal diamond." Thus, we need reconciliation and healing.

From a psychological and sociological point of view, the human person is a struggling pilgrim. We are on a journey, and the roads we travel are often arduous, if not overwhelming. Wars, injustices, and violence are but a few obstacles that make our journey so difficult. Then there are the interior battles that many of us struggle with in low self-esteem or various forms of emotional distress. On the positive side are such things as strong families and communities that support us on the journey of life. Add to this healthy educational institutions and just governments and we see that much help is available. It is when individuals and communities become self-absorbed that sin does its violence. The common good is no longer served and suffering is intensified.

Given these many perspectives, is there a reasonable and clear Christian anthropology? Here is a passage from the writings of Father James Bacik in which he gives a summary statement about the human person as reflected in the works of Karl Rahner, S.J. Father Rahner was one of the greatest and most respected theologians of the twentieth century and a major influence at Vatican Council II. Here is Father Bacik's synopsis of Rahner's anthropology:

Rahner's whole theological system is rooted in his understanding of the human person as spirit in the world. As spiritual persons, we have infinite longings and are positively oriented to the Mystery we call God. We hunger and thirst for a love that is imperishable and for knowledge that exceeds our grasp. We have the ability to reach out to others and to withdraw into the solitude of our own hearts. Our pilgrim journey brings us a diverse mixture of pleasure and pain, success and failure, satisfaction and disappointment. Along with our infinite longings, we experience our overwhelming finitude. We know physical fatigue, emotional upset, moral failure, intellectual limitation and religious dryness. In all aspects of our lives, we experience both the power of divine grace and the threat of sin and guilt. In our better moments, we hear a call to develop our potential, to deepen our relationships, and to serve the common good. As Christians we believe that God calls us to put on the mind of Christ and to be more responsive to the promptings of the Spirit.[1]

A Midrash:
The Battle between Sin and Grace

As human persons we have much in common with the animal world. In fact, many animals far exceed us in the sensory life: a dog's power of smell, a cheetah's speed, a hawk's eyesight, and the list goes on. It is precisely as spiritual beings that our existence transcends that of our fellow creatures. Two things in particular are unique to the human person: love and knowledge. And it is in both of these areas that we struggle because our longings for loving relationship and wisdom are infinite while our capacities are so finite.

Sin finds expression here when, through lack of humility, we seek more than we can attain. Goethe's *Faust* is a classic example of those longings gone awry. While not denying that our desires for knowledge and love are infinite, our challenge is to embrace our human condition and not attempt to play God. Easier said than done. There does seem to be a hole in the bucket and our limited affection and knowledge does not satisfy. We can quite easily become cynical, bitter, and sulky as we refuse our assigned role in life.

Another dimension in the nature of the human person, in Rahner's vision, is a twofold ability: reaching out and reaching in. We all have an inner and an outer world. Various personality types are called extroverts; others, introverts, depending upon the amount of time and energy we devote to the outer or inner realms. A healthy balance between the two offers the best possibility for some peace.

Sin and the need for reconciliation appear when extremes are the order of the day. Reaching out to others in service is a significant part of the Christian vocation. Spending time in solitude, silence, and reflection is another element in nurturing growth and the development of our full potential. But when one spends no time in graced solitude or when one gives no attention or energy to the needs of others, then we must examine what is going on and seek to "reconcile" these components of our life.

Ambiguity and its sibling, ambivalence, mark our Christian anthropology. Life is messy; life is not neat and clean. There is a great mixture of ups and downs, joys and sorrows, victories and defeats. It was this milieu that Jesus entered and it was to this environment that the Lord brought his healing balm.

You win some; you lose some. Such is life. It is indeed a mixture of all kinds of experiences. We need to give our "fiat" as Mary did, saying "yes" to our essential creaturehood. We are radically indigent, and this poverty of spirit has the capacity of throwing us into the arms of a providential God. The Lord remains with us in our successes or failures, in our happiness and sadness. The challenge is not to allow the vicissitudes of life to lead us into spiritual amnesia. God is with us through all of life, be it good or bad times, sickness or health. We are all tempted to doubt God when things do not go our way or when the disharmony of history is overwhelming. Much grace is needed lest we sin by forgetting God's abiding, loving presence.

The human person is made with infinite longings; the human person is made with limitations and finitudes that thwart our insatiable hungers. Frustration reigns when our expectations are out of line with reality. To expect more than is possible takes us down that slippery road of neurosis. False expectations can lead to sin when anger sweeps through the soul, an anger at God for constructing a world of such complexity.

Life is messy; life is not neat and clean. There is a great mixture of ups and downs, joys and sorrows, victories and defeats.

Without exception, every person is plunged into a universal human condition regardless of religion or race, period of history or personality type. Everyone must deal with physical, psychological, moral, intellectual, and spiritual facts: tiredness, distress, sin, limited IQs, and apathy. No exceptions; no exemptions. From the positive point of view this universal reality offers us the possibility of compassion. Our experience is similar to that of others, and we can understand and appreciate that from the inside. On the negative side, we constantly try to deny our humanity and to transcend our God-given creaturehood. It is here that we enter the arena of sin: a playing of perfection, a denial of our sinfulness, an unwillingness to humbly accept our finitude.

Finally, according to Rahner as summarized by Father Bacik, a Christian anthropology must speak directly of grace and sin. Just as grace is offered at all times so too must we deal with the threat of sin. Every hour we decide whether we will do God's will or our own. God constantly invites us to deepen our relationship with him; we constantly face forces that would put us at the center of the universe. The Christian life is one of responding to the movements of the Spirit and being configured to the person of Jesus. Sin is saying no to the action of grace and refusing to put on the mind and heart of Christ.

God's Image and Likeness

The question of identity is eternal. Every individual and every age must deal with the "who am I" query. In our contemporary culture we tend to express that identity as autonomous creatures. Our Christian ancestors would have none of this. Our identity is directly and ultimately related to the mystery of God. We are made in God's image and likeness, and until we comprehend this fact our self-knowledge will be incomplete and erroneous.

The mystery of the human person is grounded in the mystery of God. The God revealed in Jesus is a God of love, compassion, and forgiveness. Indelibly imprinted on our souls is an image of the God that no one, no action can destroy. This is who we are. Whether or not that image ever becomes developed and expressed is another question. Although made in the likeness of God, we can choose to be "unlike" God, though the image remains. Sin tarnishes our likeness to God and conceals the image.

In the sacrament of reconciliation we come before God as we are. The elements of "unlikeness" are to be named and presented before the confessor: elements such as meanness, indifference, injustice, dishonesty, impurity. These actions and attitudes contradict our deepest reality. In expressing sorrow and making a firm resolution, we seek once again to recommit ourselves to living in accord with our essential identity: creatures made in the image and likeness of a loving, compassionate, forgiving God.

Meditations: Prayerful Ponderings of the Human Person

Nelson Mandela, the first black president of South Africa, who endured almost thirty years of political imprisonment, offered this reflection in his inaugural address:

> Our deepest fear is not that we are inadequate. Our deepest fear is that we are powerful beyond measure. It is our light not our darkness that frightens us. We ask ourselves, "Who am I to be brilliant, gorgeous, talented, fabulous?" Your playing small doesn't serve the world. There's nothing enlightened about shrinking so that other people won't feel insecure around you. We are born to manifest the glory of God that is within us. It's not just in some of us. It's in everyone, and, as we let our light shine, we unconsciously give other people permission to do the same. As we are liberated from our own fear, our presence automatically liberates others.

It is no surprise that the disposition of fear is mentioned so often in Scripture and that God keeps telling us not to be afraid. This theme permeates the gospel because fear is such a universal and pervasive reality. It takes courage to take ownership and responsibility for the gifts God has given us. God's glory, the imprint of his image, is upon everyone and our challenge is to let our light shine. Sin hides our talents and gifts under the bushel basket; grace empowers us to put our talents on the lampstand and let them burn brightly to help others on their perilous journey.

William James, an American psychologist and philosopher of great renown, speaks powerfully about the enigma of the human person. We do have the power to change and to be transformed; we all have to struggle with the multiple levels of physical, psychological, and spiritual components of our personality; we need to be in touch with resources that often are far beyond our rational self:

> We have no right to speak of human crocodiles and boa-constrictors as of fixedly incurable beings. We know not the complexities of personality, the smouldering emotional fires, the other facets of the character-polyhedron, the resources of the subliminal region.[2]

In seeking reconciliation, we need to have a healthy self-compassion. We are complex creatures and the diverse levels of our personalities defy complete understanding. Thus, in dealing with others and ourselves, we must be careful not to label and be dismissive. We know not the dark regions of the human heart. Honesty demands that each of us acknowledge that we have dark regions in our own heart that we pray others won't label or exclude us for possessing. Jesus urges us to be as compassionate as his heavenly Father.

Let us listen attentively to other wisdom figures who help us understand that we are made in the image and likeness of God, who help us understand that we are a mystery and are involved in a lifelong process of coming to self-knowledge and conversion:

> How immensely much is... in a single human being! How much is contained in a being that possesses consciousness and is pervaded by the light of reason, that is endowed with a capacity for love and for knowledge, that is free, and a bearer of moral values; a being which, in contradistinction to all others, is not merely a vestige but an image of God. (Dietrich von Hildebrand)[3]

> If we accept that the human being has been created by God, endowed with freedom, and made responsible for his or her own life, and even if we accept in addition that there are limits to freedom and responsibility, and especially that through the weakness of sin no human being can attain wholeness of life through effort that is unaided by divine grace — even Kant in spite of his insistence on autonomy conceded as much — yet we are still bound to say that there must be some human contribution to the work of redemption, even if it is no more than responsive and never of equal weight with the grace of God. (John Macquarrie)[4]

> It is when we try to grapple with another man's intimate need that we perceive how incomprehensible, wavering, and misty are the beings that share with us the sight of the stars and the warmth of the sun. (Joseph Conrad)[5]

Fundamental to modernity is this new sense of what it means to be a human being: a separate and autonomous self, detached and free, and ultimately alone. He is the fruit of an evolution that has gone on for centuries, in which social bonds have been dissolved, and privacy has become possible and an ideal. He has been the hero since the time of Descartes. We can see him in every American western, a lonely figure. (Timothy Radcliffe, O.P.)[6]

In the face of a multitude — real or imaginary — it is easy to forget the needs of each one in the multitude. Face to face with one man, we cannot forget, we cannot fail to know, what he wants and what he needs. For he has a life like our own, woven of joys and sorrows, anxieties and fears, work and loves. He has a wife and children, or else the problem of living without them. He needs to think, to learn, to have poetry in his life; to see an inward meaning in the things of every day. He needs faith and sacraments; he needs some explanation of suffering, stimulus for courage; he needs work which will not only bring in the food for the body but will content his soul and will be the means by which his likeness to the Trinity can be restored to him. He needs a reasonable measure of solitude, and he has the right to the secrets of his own soul, the right to set his own standard, to suffer his own sorrows, and, above all, he has the right, the necessity, and the obligation to adore. (Caryll Houselander)[7]

Chapter Three

The Context for Reconciliation

I N THE FIELD OF PSYCHOLOGY, awareness of family systems is of great significance. To understand children and their attitudes and behavior, one must know something about their parents and siblings. Knowledge of the whole family is helpful in interpreting what is going on in the life of the children, for good or ill.

So, too, with the sacrament of reconciliation. It is one of seven sacraments and it finds its meaning in reference to the other six, especially the sacraments of baptism, confirmation, and Eucharist. By looking at the functions of the sacraments of initiation, we can garner deeper insights into the purpose of reconciliation.

Baptism

In baptism, the very gift of God's life is offered to us, God calls us to respond to five invitations: the call to maturity, the call to holiness, the call to community, the call to service, and the call to generosity. Whenever these calls are not heeded or thwarted by harmful attitudes or behaviors, we stand in need of forgiveness and reconciliation.

Mature Christians put on the mind and heart of Jesus. This is a lifelong process involving constant conversion. Too often, immaturity shows itself when we judge others by appearance, fail to have compassion for the suffering, become angry when our personal expectations are not met. Growing up is so much more than a physical process. Psychological and spiritual growth demand serious discipline and much grace.

This growth also calls for forgiveness. Immature people hurt others by blowing up, speaking before thinking, criticizing unfairly, failing to honor the good intentions of others, manipulating and exploiting others for our own pleasure or gain. We need to turn to the Lord for healing and for the grace to grow into the full stature of Christ.

In his autobiography, *Surprised by Joy*, the Christian writer C. S. Lewis carefully traced his growth toward maturity. With great candor and graceful style, Lewis described his gradual movement from atheism, to theism, and on to Christianity. And, along the way, he names his sinfulness and his resistance to God's graced invasions. Lewis writes: "The Prodigal Son at least walked home on his own feet. But who can duly adore the Love which will open the high gates for a prodigal who is brought in kicking, struggling, resentful, and darting his eyes in every direction for a chance of escape."[1]

A second call coming to all of us through the sacrament of baptism is the call to holiness. In fact, before any other vocation — be it a call to marriage or the single life, to ordained ministry or consecrated life — everyone, without exception, is called to a life of love. Holiness is the perfection of love. Obviously, none of us achieves that perfection completely. Our active concern for others can always be more intensive and extensive; our loving knowledge of others continues to unfold; our respect for friends and strangers needs constant expression.

When we come to the sacrament of reconciliation, we examine how well or how poorly we are doing in reference to this path of holiness. Do I respond to the needs of those around me with graciousness and generosity? Have I grown in my knowledge and love of God and others on a regular and consistent basis? Is my respect for others and for myself broad and deep, or it is narrow and confined? When the answers to these and other questions are negative, we stand in need of God's mercy and the grace offered through the sacrament of reconciliation.

Mother Teresa of Calcutta has been, for many of us, a symbol of holiness. Her love for the poorest of the poor challenges all of us to be more open to our hurting sisters and brothers. But even Mother Teresa was constantly aware that her love, profound as it was, was limited. She and her community recognized the need for daily prayer and the sacrament of reconciliation as a means of being even more loving.

In a collection of prayers and sayings, *A Gift for God*, Mother Teresa writes: "Thoughtfulness is the beginning of great sanctity. Our vocation, to be beautiful, must be full of thoughts for others."[2] Holiness is beautiful because it is radiant with love. Sin is ugly because it involves a selfishness that fails to reach out to others, especially those in need. One need but monitor one's thought patterns for an hour to see whether or not we are on the road to sanctity. Are our thoughts centered on our needs and anxieties or are we thinking of others and their welfare? Baptism calls us to the beauty of a holy life; reconciliation helps us to deal with our tendency to get wrapped up in ourselves.

Through baptism, all of us are called to community — the third call in this sacrament. In a culture of radical individualism, a culture that takes Frank Sinatra's "I Did It My Way" as its national anthem, it is difficult to hear about the common good and to perceive the solidarity of the human race. We are our brother's keeper; we are our sister's keeper. Community is all about sharing what we have and caring for those in need.

Given our social nature, we need one another and we grow by helping one another. The importance of family and friends cannot be overestimated. On this pilgrim journey, we travel together and are invited daily to participate in the joys and sorrows of our fellow pilgrims. Though some personalities are "loners," preferring solitude more than social interaction, even they need others to survive and to reach full maturity.

Sin happens when we "disconnect," when we cut ourselves off from those around us, thereby depriving them of our giftedness and, in turn, placing ourselves beyond the range of their gifts and concern. Sin separates and divides what was meant to be one and whole. Racism is a classic example of people suffering discrimination because of some extraneous factor. Though living in proximity to one another, individuals are not allowed to share in the benefits of a given culture.

In his insightful book *Sing a New Song*, Timothy Radcliffe O.P., speaks of an experience of his Dominican order:

Above all we should offer each other hope and mercy. Often we are drawn to the Order because we admire the brethren. We hope that we will become like them. Soon we will discover that they are in fact just like us, fragile, sinful and selfish. This can be a moment of profound disillusionment. I remember a novice complaining of this sad discovery. The novice master replied to him, "I am delighted to hear that you no longer admire us.

Now there is a chance that you might come to love us." The redemptive mystery of God's love is to be seen not in a community of spiritual heroes, but of brothers or sisters, who encourage each other on the journey to the Kingdom with hope and mercy.[3]

Living together has its moments of glory and its times of intense trial. Romanticism does not help. What does help is God's grace empowering us to be realistic about our gifts and limitations. We need great patience and encouragement; we need large buckets of mercy and hope.

> *One need but monitor one's thought patterns for an hour to see whether or not we are on the road to sanctity.*

"Community is the place where we lay ourselves open to genuine conversion. It is the corporate environment that preserves and nurtures the ongoing process of conversion." This statement by Jim Wallis in his *The Call to Conversion* (115) gets us to the core of the matter. Our life in community is one constant call to conversion, a turning away from selfishness to radical concern for others. Though difficult and challenging, it is the source of tremendous joy and peace.

The fourth call that comes to everyone through the sacrament of baptism is the call to serve. Jesus is clear in word and action that service is at the heart of his mission. In its most radical form, service or ministry is the bringing together of gifts and needs. A doctor is skilled in healing; the hurting are brought to her for assistance. The student is in want of knowledge; teachers instruct and share their wisdom. The international community needs diplomats of integrity and courage; a person like Dag Hammarskjöld steps forward and serves. Yet service and ministry have a built-in mutuality: those who serve are also being served by those they help. Have not doctors often left the bedside of a dying patient having experienced a graced nobility in how that patient has embraced his or her condition? Have not teachers often been enriched in wisdom and knowledge through the insights of their students? Have not pastors been nourished in their spiritual lives by the prayers and dedication of their parishioners?

This call to serve is not always heeded. Gifted people sometimes refuse to embrace their giftedness or are unwilling to use their blessings for the well-being of others. The light is put under the bushel basket; the talent is buried in some apparently safe place. The full life that Jesus came to bring is short-circuited when we refuse to serve. Let's call this sin: the possession of talents and gifts that are not used. Goethe's poetic insight is worth pondering: "What is not used is but a burden to bear." And, not infrequently, depression quickly follows upon this non-use.

There is a startling line in John Macquarrie's *Principles of Christian Theology:* "The ministry of reconciliation is the ministry of responding to those in need, and without this, any other kind of ministry is empty" (423). Service is quite simple in its definition: responding to the needs of others. The story of the good Samaritan has captured the imagination of people for thousands of years because it is so clear as to what is being asked of us. Whoever is in need is our neighbor and has a claim on our time, our talent, and yes, our treasure. And we must add that hopefully the service is rendered with joy, for if it is not, according to the great Hindu

leader Gandhi, neither the servant nor the one served will find
joy or peace.

Besides the calls to maturity, holiness, community, and
service, baptism involves the vocation of generosity. The
underpinning of this vocation lies in the fact that we are
gifted. God has given us the gift of life, of freedom, and so
much more. Hopefully, we are grateful and refuse to take any
gift for granted. If this sense of gratitude is deep and habitual,
this thankfulness overflows into a life of generosity. We begin
to image our God, who is a Giver. We begin to emulate the
Holy Spirit, who is always giving.

This call to generosity can, like all the other calls in baptism, go unheeded. We tend to take things for granted or begin
to hoard our time and talent and limited resources. The acquisitive spirit in the human heart seeks excessive security.
Accumulation rather than distribution becomes the way of
life. In a short time our possessions possess us and we lose
our freedom. All of this — the acquisitive spirit, the excessive
search for security, the lack of trust in God's providence —
needs to be named and healed. It is in the sacrament of reconciliation that we can bring light and grace to these dark
dimensions of our life.

Giving has its own language and one that is both simple
and complex. In Iain Pears's novel *The Dream of Scipio,* the
author offers this philosophical reflection on gift giving:

> Ever since men began to study themselves, that gift has
> attracted the fascinated attention of those who see the
> practice as one of the strangest and most complex forms
> of communication — particularly, but not solely, human.
> When to give, how to give, what to give; these are
> complex matters, and getting the practice right requires

subtlety and care if it is not to miss the mark. In many ways Oliver, though still so young, had the easiest task, as he lived in an age when the language of gift giving was understood, with a straightforward grammar and simple syntax.[4]

There is a need to recapture "the language of gift giving" since our Western culture has nurtured for years the grammar and syntax of acquisition. Moreover, there are segments of our culture that are characterized by "entitlement." Demanding rights has outpaced our sense of duty and responsibility. Again we need conversion. We are called to turn from a lifestyle of having (and demanding) to a lifestyle of giving (and responsibility).

Thomas Merton, the prolific spiritual writer and Trappist, wrote: "There are three gifts I have received for which I can never be grateful enough: first, my Catholic faith; second, my monastic vocation; third, my calling to be a writer and share my beliefs with others." Here is an attitude that expresses mature discipleship. Our gratitude can never measure up to the gifts given. Yet in a humble and honest way, we gradually become more and more a Eucharistic people, a community of thanksgiving, by reflecting upon and responding to God's gracious generosity to us.

Confirmation

In the sacrament of baptism, our life in Christ begins; in the sacrament of confirmation, that life is strengthened through the gift of the Holy Spirit. Before the candidates are confirmed, the bishop leads the community in this beautiful prayer:

> All powerful God, Father of our Lord Jesus
>   Christ,
> by water and the Holy Spirit
> you freed your sons and daughters from sin
> and gave them new life.
> Send your Holy Spirit upon them
> to be their helper and guide.
> Give them the spirit of wisdom and
>   understanding,
> the spirit of right judgment and courage,
> the spirit of knowledge and reverence.
> Fill them with the spirit of wonder and awe in
>   your presence.
> We ask this through Christ our Lord. Amen.[5]

It is through the gift of the Spirit of Jesus and the Father that Christians are enlightened, enkindled, and empowered. That seeing, loving, and acting is directed to the doing of God's will and the building of God's Kingdom. That same Holy Spirit helps us to see our sinfulness, to challenge us when we are unloving, and to judge those actions that are contrary to God's designs.

It is in the sacrament of confirmation that the Christian is sent forth on mission, the mission of furthering the Kingdom of God. Thus, when the Christian fails to take on that mission there is need for forgiveness, a need for God's mercy. Pope John XXIII, in his revolutionary encyclical *Pacem in Terris* (1962), describes the Kingdom of God and thus, the mission of the Christian community, in terms of peace. The risen Lord, on appearing to the frightened disciples, exclaimed: "Peace be with you. Receive the Holy Spirit." This self-giving gift of God empowered the disciples to go forth with courage to bring peace to a broken world.

But John XXIII went on to speak of four qualities of God's Kingdom that make peace possible: truth, charity, freedom, and justice. Peace is shattered by lies and indifference, by enslavement and injustice. Every person is on a pilgrimage of peace, either as agents of God's Kingdom or channels of chaos and discord (and sometimes both in the same day). Within this understanding of the mission given in confirmation we see how confirmation is related to the sacrament of reconciliation. We stand in need of healing to the extent that the four principles of God's Kingdom — truth, charity, freedom, and justice — are not being lived. A brief examination of each of these four ingredients of the Kingdom links confirmation to the grace of reconciliation.

Truth! The Holy Spirit offers us the gift of truth, to live in the reality of things. Too often we live a lie or with illusions. The great truths of our faith are the mysteries of creation, redemption, and sanctification: the truth that we are created and totally dependent upon our loving Creator; the truth that we all stand in need of redemption through the blood of Christ, a redemption necessitated by sin, personal and collective; and, the truth that the Holy Spirit has been sent into the world to renew all creation and to restore us to friendship with God.

But rather than live in the light of these truths, we may choose darkness and doubt. To accept our creaturehood and poverty of spirit is no easy task; to realize that we are in need of redemption calls for humility and brutal honesty; to embrace our need for the Spirit to transform our minds and hearts into a new creation makes us indebted for life. It is no surprise that the truths of the gospel are often rejected because they change our self-understanding and the very meaning of our lives.

Raïssa Maritain, the wife of the noted philosopher Jacques Maritain, describes "the essential thing" in her life:

> But before all else, I had to make sure of the essential thing: the possession of the truth about God, about myself, and about the world. It was, I knew, the necessary foundation for my life; I could not, without letting the ground be washed away from under me, give up the pursuit of its discovery. Such was my deep instinct. And by assiduous work must I prepare myself to receive the hard secrets of the Spirit. All the rest, I thought, would follow, would come in its time — music, the sweetness of the world, the happiness of life.[6]

This is indeed arduous work made even more difficult in our day because of pluralism, the multiplication of various belief systems. Confusion reigns in many quarters, and agnostics, by definition, have given up the possibility of finding the truth.

When we encounter the Lord in the sacrament of reconciliation we are again given the truth that God is merciful. In hearing the words of absolution we are reminded time and time again of the paschal mystery and how the Holy Spirit was sent into the world for the forgiveness of sin. Here is the essential thing — the truth of God's love, the truth that we are forgiven, the truth that the world is renewed and restored through grace. Here is the truth that sets us free.

Charity! There is no peace without love. It is when charity reigns in the hearts of people that the Kingdom of God is truly among us. And this love, this charity, is both demanding and joyful for it flowers into oneness with God and unity among people. In confirmation, the Spirit of love is offered and those who are disposed will enter into a deep process of transformation. It is a love that will confront our innate selfishness; it is a love that, like truth, will set us free.

In our confirmation call to further the Kingdom we come to realize the need for "real supernatural charity." Listen to the Anglican spiritual writer Evelyn Underhill as she points out the demands of this deep love: "That is real supernatural charity. It is a call to love and save not the nice but the nasty, not the lovable but the unlovely, the hard, the narrow, and the embittered, and the tiresome, who are so much worse."[7] How easy it is to walk away and say that we don't need the abuse from another. Yet it is precisely here that Jesus provides his witness by loving his enemies as he hung upon the cross, loving Peter even in his betrayal, loving the tax collectors and sinners as they sat together at table.

At the heart of the sacrament of reconciliation is the mystery of love. All sin is, in some sense, a refusal to love or to be loved; all grace is about love being offered and embraced. Since all the sacraments are encounters with the risen Christ, all the sacraments are encounters with Love-made-flesh. It is Jesus who forgives us and implants divine charity deep within our souls.

Romano Guardini, in his classic *The Lord*, brings great clarity to the necessity of God's grace if we are to be loving:

Genuine love of neighbor is impossible through human strength alone; it necessitates something new which comes from God and which surpasses the logic of mere human differentiation or unification: the love of the Holy Spirit among men. Christian love does not attempt to fuse the I and the you, or to impose upon them an attitude of selflessness that would annihilate the individual.

It is the disposition of reciprocal openness and autonomy together, that simultaneous intimacy and dignity which comes from the Holy Ghost.[8]

So once again, the growth of the Kingdom comes both through the gift of the Spirit in confirmation and the Spirit's working through reconciliation. The power to love is an ongoing gift and its constant renewal is available to all those who confess their need for divine help.

Freedom! One of the most precious and fragile gifts from God is our freedom. Every day we are invited to make choices that will further God's design. However, rather than walking the road of love, compassion, and forgiveness, we can choose to travel in the opposite direction. Instead of life, we choose death; instead of love, we remain indifferent or even opt for hatred; instead of light, we journey into darkness and chaos. Freedom is indeed a matter of life or death.

The poet Goethe was right: "Freedom and life are earned by those alone / Who conquer them each day anew." Freedom is a gift and a responsibility. Gifts have to be received and nurtured if they are to reach maturity. Gifts can be wasted or squandered, leaving us depressed and without meaning. Each day we must awake and decide to choose life and not death, to live life to the full and not in half measures.

The question of freedom is a question of destiny. Therefore, it is a question of obedience or disobedience: will we do what God asks of us or will we go our own way? In *Mere Christianity,* C. S. Lewis puts the cards on the table:

It [freedom] is something they can freely give Him or freely refuse Him. Will they, or will they not, turn to Him and thus fulfill the only purpose for which they were created? Their free will is trembling inside them like the needle of a compass. But this is a needle that can choose. It can point to its true North; but it need not. Will the needle swing round, and settle, and point to God?[9]

Jesus came to set us free from both sin and death. It is through the sacrament of reconciliation that we encounter once again the gift of freedom, a gift, that when used appropriately, furthers both God's plan and our own happiness and peace. Paradoxically, it is in obedience that our freedom is both maintained and grown.

Often we find in literature a great deal of spiritual wisdom. In Dostoevsky's *The Brothers Karamazov* we are offered this insight:

> Obedience, fasting, and prayer are laughed at, yet only through them lies the way to real, true freedom. I cut off my superfluous and unnecessary desires, I subdue my proud and wanton will and chastise it with obedience, and with God's help I attain freedom of spirit and with it spiritual joy.[10]

The assignment of a penance in the sacrament of reconciliation often relates directly to the path to true freedom. The confessor might direct the penitent to a specific way of following a commandment or encourage the penitent to some form of asceticism or mortification, or point the penitent to regular prayer. All of these instructions point to the freedom of the spirit and, as Dostoevsky comments, even to spiritual joy. If we are honest, all of us have to struggle with unnecessary desires, a wanton will, and outright disobedience. Sin attacks our freedom and subverts the experience of joy.

Justice! In the Roman synod of bishops in 1971, we read that "action on behalf of justice and participation in the transformation of the world fully appear to us as a constitutive part of preaching the gospel." Our Christian life is intimately linked with justice and transformation. We cannot avoid the call to bring God's justice and peace to a broken world, including our own broken hearts.

God's Kingdom of peace has this fourth essential ingredient. There is no peace without justice, just as there is no peace without truth, charity, and freedom. These elements are part of a family system, interconnected virtues that lead to fullness of life. Justice is fundamental to the moral life and also to an authentic spiritual life. Whenever the moral claim to do or have something, be it a claim to education or housing, health care or religious liberty, respect or employment, is denied, we are involved in sin. More, whenever we fail to fulfill our duties and obligations, the flip side to justice's rights, we need forgiveness.

The Persian proverb — "To spare the ravening leopard is an act of injustice to the sheep" — points out one of the dilemmas of justice. Can we "justify" killing the leopard to save the sheep? Is it morally permissible to use force and violence in attempting to balance the scale of justice? What is to be done when an aggressor attacks the innocent? Justice, like truth, charity, and freedom, is a value threatened by many forces. The great moral people of history have agonized over these complex moral issues.

One example will suffice. In World War II, the Lutheran theologian Dietrich Bonhoeffer (1906–45) took part in a conspiracy to overthrow Hitler and his regime. Bonhoeffer was keenly aware of the injustices that the Nazis perpetrated on the Jewish people and so many others. After much prayer and deliberation, Bonhoeffer made the difficult decision to use violence to stop the injustice. The conspiracy failed. Bonhoeffer was captured and executed in April of 1945. His final message was: "This is the end, for me the beginning of life."

As we examine our own conscience in light of the call to be a just person and a just society, we realize that the promotion and protection of rights are often wanting. At times we fail to respect the good name of others or fail to fulfill our duties toward family or state. At the societal level, we live in a culture where abortion has been legalized, denying the right to life to the unborn. Our society struggles with other major moral issues all centered around the virtue of justice: euthanasia, stem cell research, war, capital punishment, and the list goes on. Sin is the denial of rights; sin is the failure to do our duties. We all stand in need of God's mercy and forgiveness.

Eucharist

The Eucharist, or Mass, makes Jesus present in word and sacrament. Just as it is Christ who baptizes and confirms us in the faith, so too it is in the Eucharist that Jesus comes to nourish and strengthen us for the journey. Three brief comments might help us to see the relationship between the Eucharist and the sacrament of reconciliation.

Penitential Rite

After the processional song and greeting of the assembled community, the presider of the Eucharist leads the faithful in one of the most beautiful and meaningful prayers of the church, the "Confiteor." When this confession flows from the heart, it disposes the community to hear God's word and to celebrate with reverence the mysteries of our faith. Prayerfully ponder this rich oration:

> I confess to almighty God,
> and to you, my brothers and sisters,
> that I have sinned through my own fault
> in my thoughts and in my words,
> in what I have done,
> and in what I have failed to do;
> and I ask blessed Mary, ever virgin,
> all the angels and saints,
> and you, my brothers and sisters,
> to pray for me to the Lord our God.

Admission of sin is very freeing; to receive the help of Mary, the angels and saints, and all of our sisters and brothers, is very consoling. We do not face our sin alone. It is within the communion of saints that we approach our loving and merciful God.

God's Word

The liturgy of the word puts us in touch with the mind and heart of God. Revelation is the grace that opens for us the mystery of God's love and mercy. That word is also a judgment, calling us to face the dark side of our life. That word is a healing balm, as we come to recognize our insufficiency and absolute dependence upon God's mercy. Scripture has tremendous power to change our self-understanding and the meaning of life. It helps us to name both grace and sin. To ponder God's word with reverence and devotion is to already experience new life.

In his excellent work *Asking the Fathers,* Aelred Squire comments:

> We too often fail to realize that one of the primary purposes of holy Scriptures, considered as a vital whole, is to show man to himself, as he was made and as he has become, as he acts and reacts in relation to his maker, with nothing left out. Hence the violence and crudity and sensuality that God there pushes in front of our noses, even if we would, to our very great danger, prefer to turn away.[11]

A central element in the sacrament of reconciliation is self-knowledge. To come to an accurate assessment of who we are is a long and difficult journey. We need mirrors to reflect back to us qualities and traits that remain obscure until named. Scripture names; Scripture tells stories; Scripture holds that mirror before us until we learn to say: "I am the man; I am the woman!" Add to this proclamation of God's word a good, insightful homily and we have the opportunity of growing in self-awareness and in the awareness of a God of love and mercy.

In *A Community of Character,* Stanley Hauerwas writes: "For the scripture forms a society and sets an agenda for its life that requires nothing less than trusting its existence to the God found through the stories of Israel and Jesus" (66). We need but read the Beatitudes to see the agenda Jesus holds. We need but read the stories of Moses and King David, of Mary and Joseph, of Peter and Paul, to see the centrality of God in the formation of a religious society and the call to trust in divine providence.

When our spirituality is rooted in God's word we have a resource for making the sacrament of reconciliation a powerful means of growth. The Bible reveals God's mercy and love; the Bible makes manifest our sin and its horrendous consequences. Since the revision of the liturgy after the Second Vatican Council, God's word has taken on an integral role in the celebration of the sacrament.

Eucharistic Prayer (III)

Three brief meditations highlight again the link between the Eucharist and reconciliation:

> Take this, all of you, and drink from it:
> this is the cup of my blood,
> the blood of the new and everlasting covenant.
> It will be shed for you and for all
> so that sins may be forgiven.

Jesus' self-offering won for us our salvation. In shedding his blood, Jesus broke the bonds of sin and destroyed the power of sin. The price of our salvation is incredibly high. Even higher, is the mystery of God's love.

> Look with favor on your Church's offering,
> and see the Victim whose death has reconciled us to
>   yourself.
> Grant that we, who are nourished by his body and
>   blood,
> may be filled with his Holy Spirit,
> and become one body, one spirit in Christ.

Not only does the sacrifice of Christ reconcile us to the Father and the community, but the Holy Spirit is given so that we might experience unity. A deep faith regarding the indwelling of God's Spirit gives us a confidence and courage that no danger can overcome.

> Lord, may this sacrifice,
> which has made our peace with you,
> advance the peace and salvation of all the world.

Once again we return to that farewell gift of peace. Through the sacrifice of Jesus we are offered not only the grace of salvation but the peace that is beyond all understanding.

Chapter Four ─────────────────────────

The Mystery of Sin

> Have mercy on me, O God,
> according to your steadfast love;
> according to your abundant mercy
> blot out my transgressions. (Ps. 51:1)

G RACE AND SIN are two realities that demand serious, prayerful reflection. Grace has to do with God's gifts of light, love, and life. Sin deals with darkness, destruction, and death. Every day we have to decide which road we will travel. Will it be the road of obedience to God's will or the road of transgressions? All of us have known both paths; all of us have tasted the joy of obedience and the shame and guilt of sin.

Several metaphors might help us "see" what sin is and what it does. One image is that of an ingrown toenail. Just to say the words makes us squirm. But the metaphor pictures for us what St. Augustine thought was at the heart of sinfulness: *curvatus in se,* a turning in upon oneself. Sin, in all of its forms, tells of the disease of narcissism, that excessive self-preoccupation. Here time, talent, and energies are consumed by one's own narrow ego and are not used to meet the needs of others.

> Is there a law of gravity,
> psychological in nature,
> pulling us down,
> deep down into ourselves?

When Newton saw the apple fall,
did he say *curvatus in se*?
Surely, the tree was not to blame,
nor the west wind,
not even the child Eve,
hungry for knowledge.

"Gravity made me do it,"
the sinner says.

To which another voice responds:
"Grace, not gravity,
is stronger by far
deserving priority of place."[1]

A second metaphor for sin is poison ivy. Sin causes pain. Sin, like all evil, injures life and fractures community. But sin goes even deeper, for it not only disrupts external relationships but, like a deadly poison, infiltrates our inner life and damages three vital organs: the mind, the heart, and the imagination. Sin distorts truth; sin hardens our emotional life; sin brings a plethora of images that misguide and confuse us. Sin, like poison ivy, causes an itchy uneasiness.

A third metaphor describing another dimension of sin is cancer. Sin is a spiritual cancer that can lead to immense suffering, even death. Physical cancer has diverse causes and multiple effects. So, too, cancer of the soul, that is, sinfulness. Eventually, it is a sickness that demands radical treatment. The Anglican poet George Herbert describes God not only as Creator, Redeemer, and Sanctifier in his classic poem "Trinity Sunday," but also as a Purger. And this purging is done out of love. The poet prays:

> Purge all my sins done heretofore:
> For I confess my heavy score,
> And I will strive to sin no more.[2]

Some may think a surgeon cruel as he takes in hand the scalpel. But not so. The Divine Physician, out of love and mercy, cuts away those attitudes and behaviors that eat away at the mystery of life. Though the surgery is initially painful, in the end we are grateful.

Genus/Species

It is important that we recognize the distinction between sinfulness and sin. Sinfulness is the genus, a basic orientation away from God, a turning from light to darkness. Sin, in contrast to sinfulness, is an individual act or abiding attitude that chooses death over life. Sin comes in a variety of species.

Sinfulness is a way of leaning into life. It is that radical disposition that prefers doing one's own will rather than God's will. St. Augustine wrote of this condition in his classic *Confessions*. Here we see a soul that lived in confusion, unrest, and hostility. Eventually, through the prayers of Monica, Augustine's mother, and through the help of the great bishop Ambrose, God liberated Augustine and set the future bishop of Hippo on the road to freedom, though Augustine struggled throughout his life with the condition of sinfulness.

By contrast, sin takes on concrete form: the lie is told, the money is stolen, the person is manipulated, the parent is dishonored. The list is long and painful. Sin injures, disrupts, breaks apart, festers — sin is ugly. Within our Catholic tradition, there are seven kinds (species) of sin that have deep roots in our human nature. Thus, they are called capital sins because from them come individual deeds that thwart the coming of God's Kingdom. We need to ponder the nature of these capital sins and examine our conscience in light of their destructive force.

Pride

Pride, for all its tragedy, is also quite comical. Aesop's proverb captures the foolishness of pride. The fly upon the chariot wheel comments: "What dust we raise." Pride arrogates to itself an attribute, achievement, or gift that ultimately comes from God. It is like the peacock that cannot help but strut around the barnyard in all its feathered beauty thinking that the gift of its beauty resides in itself. This makes pride so laughable — and, so sad, for it takes the prideful fly, bird, or person out of the realm of truth and plunges them into darkness.

Sin distorts truth; sin hardens our emotional life; sin brings a plethora of images that misguide and confuse us. Sin, like poison ivy, causes an itchy uneasiness.

Humility is the grace needed here. Humility is to live in the truth of things. When we see things rightly, we realize that all is gift, that we are radically indigent, that awareness of our fundamental poverty should keep head bowed, knee bent. Brigid E. Herman captures well the essence of humility. She writes: "Humility, indeed, is simply a sense of reality and proportion. It is grounded upon a knowledge of the truth about ourselves and about God."[3]

In preparing for the sacrament of reconciliation, we might ask: Do I consider myself better and superior to others because of intelligence, beauty, or social status? Do I look down on others who lack social skills or because they are of a different ethnic or religious background? Am I humble? Do I live in the truth of things? Do I attribute every gift to God and acknowledge God as the source of every blessing? Do I resent those who do not recognize me or who fail to appreciate my talents? Am I arrogant in word or looks?

Someone once wrote that a certain person was the only individual who could strut sitting down. This captures well the core of pride: strutting. Thank goodness that just around the corner a banana peel waits.

Greed/Avarice

There seems to be a hole in the bucket. No matter how much we have, be it money, power, sex, food, or prestige, there never seems to be enough. A basic insecurity remains that cries out: *"More!"* The word "enough" is missing from our contemporary lexicon.

Greed is the label assigned to that inner disposition and external acquisition that fails to know proper limits. In the animal world, the pig is a symbol of wanton intake. The insatiable hunger for food, money, or whatever stems from a deep sense of emptiness. If only we could fill up, all would be well, happiness would be ours. But there is a hole in the bucket and, as we all know, shortly after replenishing our stomach with food and our wallet with money, the old emptiness and insecurity return, making us scramble for a new supply despite the fact that the bank account is heftier and the scale registers additional poundage.

St. John of the Cross, a doctor of the church, offers this reflection on greed: "These, precisely, are the greedy. Their appetite and joy is already so extended and dispersed among creatures — and with such anxiety — that they cannot be satisfied. The more their appetite and thirst increases, the further they regress from God, the fount which alone can satisfy them."[4]

The grace needed here is moderation, along with the gift of clarity to know what is sufficient and then to act on that knowledge. Saying no to greed — the "more" — demands discipline and determination. "That's enough" is a constant refrain in the soul that knows freedom and is free from enslavements and addictions. And when discipline is present and operating, joy is not far behind.

In preparing for the sacrament of reconciliation, we might ask: How much is enough in every area of my life? In looking at my finances, or lifestyle, could I be accused of greed by an objective observer? Do I have the ability to say "no" to unnecessary things and substances? Do I have the ability to distinguish between wants and needs? What do I see in the eyes of greedy people? In those who know moderation? What role does sacrifice play in my life? How wide is the eye of a needle?

Lust

Lust is the uncontrolled, undisciplined hunger for sensual satisfaction. Sexual lust is manipulative and exploitive. People are used, indeed abused, in that they are treated as objects for another's pleasure. Lust denies the human dignity of both the victim and the perpetrator. It violates our basic humanity. In the novel *The Diary of a Country Priest,* we read: "Yet whosoever has experienced sin, with its parasitic growth, must know that lust is forever threatening to stifle virility as well as intelligence."[5]

Chastity is an ordered, disciplined existence in the realm of sexuality. Chastity keeps sexual energies in check. Paradoxically, chastity is both liberating and joyful. By contrast, lust fosters enslavement and results in a deep sadness. Chaste people live in mutual respect, and the byproduct of this love and respect is the gift of peace.

In preparing for the sacrament of reconciliation, we might ask: What is my understanding of the gift of sexuality? How do I channel my sexual energies? In relating to others, do I treat them as objects to be used or as beings possessing human dignity? Do I expose myself to forms of entertainment that fill the imagination with a distorted view of human sexuality? What value do I assign to chastity, to the grace of purity? Does my language respect human sexuality? How do I deal with sexual fantasies? What does God's word have to say about lust?

Anger/Wrath

Anger is an ambiguous emotion. On the one hand, there is a just anger that arises when injustice is done and the human spirit is stirred to wrath. In fact, not to become angry at injustice could well be a moral defect. On the other hand, anger is considered a capital sin when our wrath is the result of simply not getting our way. This anger is closely allied with impatience, crankiness, and crabbiness. Our expectations are not met so we go into a snit.

In William Blake's poem "The Poison Tree," anger is compared with poison that disfigures the soul and relationships. More, this poison can be deadly in that it leads to violence. So we must be on guard lest anger become dominant in the depth of our soul.

The grace needed here is wisdom, patience, and a good portion of gratitude. Wisdom helps us to sort out which of our expectations are realistic and which are neurotic. When expectations are healthy, anger is justified. But when we discern that our expectations are off the wall, basically impossible given the human condition, then we need to have a change of attitude. Patience enables us to wait, giving both others and ourselves the time needed to mature. And gratitude helps us to avoid a life of perpetual dissatisfaction. Indeed, gratitude counters our culture of complaint that criticizes the state, the church, the culture, and everything else.

In preparing to celebrate the sacrament of reconciliation, we might ask: Are my expectations of God, life, others, and myself realistic or neurotic? How do I express my anger and what effect does that expression have on the life of those around me? Do I get angry at injustices, and if so what do I do about that? What happens when I don't get my way? Who are the people I have injured through angry words or a hostile attitude? Am I too patient with faults that can be corrected?

A practical final comment: "More anger stems from lack of sleep than from all of life's frustrations" (Don Sutton). We need energy to cope with the struggles and complexities of life. Surely, a great deal of anger arises when we lack sufficient rest. Again we see the intimate link between our physical well-being and our moral life.

Gluttony

Eating and drinking are the means of self-preservation just as sexuality is the means of continuing our species. These areas of passionate human activity demand discipline and control if personal health and the well-being of society are to be maintained. Gluttony harms our personal well-being. Overeating and immoderate drinking have consequences that also impact on the life of family and friends. Thus, the call for moderation and temperance if we are to be responsible stewards of our bodies and souls.

But there are other forms of gluttony than that of the body. Ralph Waldo Emerson, in his essay "New England Reformers," writes: "A canine appetite for knowledge was generated, which must still be fed but was never satisfied, and this knowledge, not being directed to action, never took the character of substantial, humane truth, blessing those whom it entered."[6] Thomas Merton, the Trappist monk, speaks also about "a kind of intellectual and esthetic gluttony — a high and refined and even virtuous form of selfishness."[7]

"Too much" is the problem of gluttony. The grace needed here is that of discipline. But realism forces us to deal with the powerful appetites that can overwhelm us. Thus, a number of supports are most helpful: good modeling of moderation, spiritual guidance in seeking to take control of this area of our life, counseling, if necessary. And there is an urgency here because gluttony, once entered into, can become a matter of life or death.

In preparing to receive the sacrament of reconciliation we might ask: Are my eating and drinking patterns healthy or not? How much food do I need? How much food do I take? Do I have to struggle with emotional and intellectual gluttony, wanting to obtain "too much" affection or knowledge? What role does discipline play in my life? Is fasting something the Lord is asking of me? Who models moderation for me?

Sloth

The expression "lazy as sin" captures a dimension of our moral life that is both frightening and depressing. Too easily the human spirit can be overcome by sluggishness, indolence, and inertia. There is a radical disinclination to act, and life then, literally, begins to pass us by. Sloth is a devastating sin because it easily leads to weariness of spirit and the inability to take on proper responsibility. In its deeper regions, it manifests a hopelessness or despair that life is essentially meaningless. Futility becomes one's personal philosophy.

In the book of Deuteronomy, as Moses is about to depart from his people, he cries out: "Choose life so that you and your descendants may live . . . " (Deut. 30:19b). Jesus, the new Moses, cries out in John's Gospel: "I came that they may have life, and have it abundantly" (John 10:10). Life demands the employment of energy; life demands that one develops one's potential. Laziness thwarts God's plan for fullness of life. Sluggishness will eventually lead to some form of depression. The failure to assume responsibility for oneself and for others is a refusal to do God's will.

In preparing for the sacrament of reconciliation we might ask: Do I procrastinate? Do I take care of myself physically so that I have the energy to do my duties? Is God calling me to greater discipline so that I might live a full and abundant life? How much rest do I need, do I take? How do indolence and laziness affect the lives of others? Do I establish goals and priorities that call for an energetic life?

Envy

St. Thomas Aquinas held that when we grieve instead of rejoice in another's good we commit the sin of envy. There is a resentment at seeing the possessions or advantages of others. Envy can lead to sadness and even to wishing harm to others. Obviously, the possibility of joy and peace is nonexistent when jealousy dominates the human spirit. The Germans even have a word for feeling good when those we don't like experience misfortune: *Schadenfreude!*

Much of envy is rooted in pride. Raïssa Maritain comments: "A proud man envies the superiority which surpasses him. A humble one, on the contrary, loves good wherever he finds it, and by this love, in some sense appropriates it to himself."[8] Here we have a clue about how to deal with envy: humility and love. Humility grounds us in the giftedness and limitations of our own life and hopefully an acceptance of our finite condition. Love or charity is the grace to love good, truth, and beauty wherever we find it.

In preparing to celebrate the sacrament of reconciliation we might ask: Do I wish ill of others because they are more gifted than I am? How do I deal with those who are superior to me in intellect, in charm, in sports, in wealth? How do I express envy? Do I become sad or depressed when I see others excel? Is resentment a problem for me? What are the objects of that resentment? Am I perpetually dissatisfied? Do I count my blessings?

Chapter Five ———————————————————

Principles of Reconciliation

J ESUS CAME to reconcile all creation back to the Father.
Not only did Jesus preach the message of forgiveness and
reconciliation, he lived it as witnessed on Calvary. This reconciliation is a major theme in *Secularity and the Gospel: Being
Missionaries to Our Children.* In a chapter entitled "Consenting to Kenosis, Mission of Secularity," Michael Downey
sets the framework for these reflections on the principles of
reconciliation:

> Talk of purification is not so much about the deep pu-
> rification of memories to which we are summoned — for
> our failures and neglect in mission, and for the harm that
> we have brought to persons, peoples, and cultures in the
> name of Christ and gospel. So much talk of purification
> in the church today is aimed at catharsis, cleansing, so
> that we can return to the scene, pure and strong again
> to — dare I say — pick up where we left off before the
> interruptions brought on by "the scandal" and by the
> erosion of the faith caused by secularism. Such a pu-
> rification can easily bypass the call to the deepest kind
> of forgiveness and reconciliation that is needed, with-
> out which the church — not just individuals within it —
> continues in the way of evil and sin. If the church has a
> mission to secularity, it begins anew each day by asking

forgiveness, even and especially from "godless people" and "godless nations," present and past.[1]

Principles are broad, sweeping generalizations that provide a framework for understanding and action. They propose a sense of direction and state a set of core values. It is possible to draw up principles for every major theme of Christianity, such as love, peace, prayer, and so on. Here are ten principles that guide us in our vocation to be agents of reconciliation, the essential mission of the Christian life.

1. Reconciliation Is Primarily the Work of God.

In the well-known prayer of St. Francis we pray to be instruments of God's peace. Hopefully, we come to a keen awareness that although we cooperate in bringing love and hope into the world, it is primarily the work of God. We are instruments, channels, and agents of graces. This in no way plays down the importance of our agency, but it makes us conscious that we are the branches through which God's vine, the Lord Jesus, is operative. "Without me, you can do nothing" (John 15:5b). With God, all things are possible.

Reconciliation is first and foremost God's work in our midst. Reconciliation is not conflict management in the sense of skills we learn that resolve things. There is much that is simply too big for us to manage by ourselves, for us to comprehend, let alone solve. We are agents, we are ambassadors for Christ's sake, as Paul says, when he speaks of reconciliation in 2 Corinthians 5. Second, reconciliation is not about getting over where we were and going back to what we had been before. It's about coming to a new place. Third, vocation is a call to action, a call to go out, to carry this reconciliation forward. We need to rediscover contemplative prayer — especially missionaries, who tend to be activists. If we cannot dwell in the presence of God on God's terms, how do we expect to be God's agents in this situation? How do we expect to be able to hear the woundedness, the cries of pain coming out of the wounds of others, if we have not learned how to live with our own wounds?

(Robert Schreiter)[2]

However, it is that paradox, namely, that the infinite God is intimately concerned with finite man and his finite deeds; that nothing is trite or irrelevant in the eyes of God, which is the very essence of prophetic faith.

(Abraham Heschel)[3]

By "reconciliation" is meant the activity whereby the disorders of existence are healed, its imbalances redressed, its alienations bridged over. (John Macquarrie)[4]

Prayer

Lord Jesus, give us the grace to be true to our vocation of reconciliation. Only through you can we overcome our fears in dealing with the brokenness of our lives and that of others. Send your Spirit into our hearts, transforming them by your love, so that we may join you in being healers of a broken world.

2. Reconciliation Is Grounded in Forgiveness.

When relationships are injured or broken, an essential component necessary for reunion is the grace of forgiveness. To be able to say those "simple" words "I forgive you" demands personal courage and the grace of the Holy Spirit. More, to say those "simple" words "I forgive myself" is as difficult as being reconciled with others and with God. One wonders how long it took Peter, after his betrayal of Jesus, to extend forgiveness to himself even though that look across the evening fire was a gaze of the Lord's forgiveness. Forgiveness demands a brutal honesty, a supreme courage, and a volume of grace.

> In a world and a culture that is full of wounds, anger, injustice, inequality, historical privilege, jealousy, resentment, bitterness, murder, and war, we must speak always and everywhere about forgiveness, reconciliation, and God's healing. Forgiveness lies at the center of Jesus' moral message. The litmus test for being a Christian is not whether one can say the creed and mean it, but whether one can forgive and love an enemy.
>
> (Ronald Rolheiser)[5]

> Instead of an easy concession, the Divine forgiveness makes a heroic demand upon our courage. For that forgiveness is not the easy passing of a sponge over a slate. It is a stern and painful process: it means the re-ordering of the soul's disordered love, setting right what is wrong, washing it from wickedness and cleansing it from sin.
>
> (Evelyn Underhill)[6]

> My fault is past. But, O! what form of prayer
> Can serve my turn? "Forgive me my foul murder"
> That cannot be since I am still possess'd
> Of those effects for which I did the murder,
> My crown, mine own ambition, and my queen.
>
> (William Shakespeare)[7]

Prayer

> Compassionate and merciful God, grant us the grace of forgiveness. Our thoughts, words, and deeds have injured you, others and ourselves — and our omissions as well. Send your Spirit of reconciliation into our hearts and communities so that we might share with others the grace given to us. St. Peter, intercede for us.

3. Reconciliation Is Enhanced by a Graced Sense of Sinfulness That Can Lead to a Life of Humility and Gratitude.

Philosophers distinguish between being and doing. Who we are and what we do are obviously connected, but identity is much broader than the specifics of our ethical life. The expression "hate the sin but love the sinner" captures a slice of what we are talking about. Sins are specific and concrete; sinfulness is a way of being wherein we live alienated from God and one another, indeed, from ourselves. Truth challenges us to face our sinfulness. And when this truth is soaked in grace it leads to humility and then on to gratitude. The truth does set us free. We all stand in need of redemption; awareness of this draws us into the embrace of God's mercy.

> We begin to notice, besides our particular sinful acts, our sinfulness; begin to be alarmed not only about what we do, but about what we are. That may sound rather difficult, so I will try to make it clear from my own case. When I come to my evening prayers and try to reckon up the sins of the day, nine times out of ten the most obvious one is some sin against charity: I have sulked or snapped or sneered or snubbed or stormed. (C. S. Lewis)[8]

Sin is our refusal to become who we truly are. In those moments when I kneel before God in penitence, or join with others in confession, sometimes I am aware of specific faults: unloving words, thoughtless conduct, selfish actions. I am aware of not caring enough. But chiefly I am aware of a much more subtle temptation: to settle for less than I might be. To choose the lesser good. To lack curiosity and wonder. To miss the mark because my sights are fixed too low. Not to perceive that I am "fearfully and wonderfully made" in God's image. And when I ask God to forgive me, I do so because, in settling for less than I am created to be, I know not what I do.

(Michael Mayne)[9]

[Evelyn] Underhill epitomizes what has been called the greatest female sin — the devaluation of self and the inability to love oneself. For most of her life, Underhill was unable to experience for herself what she saw so clearly in the lives of the mystics — unearned love that makes one lovable. It was her greatest failure.

(Dana Greene)[10]

Prayer

God of wisdom and compassion, grant us the grace to see ourselves as you see us. Pride would turn our eyes from the truth; stupidity blinds us to accurate self-knowledge. Empower us to name those attitudes and behaviors that separate us from you. Strengthen us with the courage to confess and repent of our sinfulness. Only then will we know the grace of peace and the beauty of your joy.

4. Reconciliation Deals with an Incredible Volume of Death and Sin but Even More with the Experience of God's Infinite Grace and Life.

Death and sin are ubiquitous. We must be careful in exposing ourselves to the dark side of life. It is dangerous for the soul. Without denying either the range or volume of sin and death, we must gaze as well upon the divine milieu. God's world is filled with grace, charged with grandeur as Gerard Manley Hopkins sees it. Love and life are even more ubiquitous than hatred and death. In experiencing reconciliation, we must focus deeply upon God's mercy lest our awareness of sin overwhelm us. Keeping a graced perspective is essential to a healthy and holy life.

> Human existence is so deeply wounded and threatened by sin that the passage from fear to trust, from hostility to love, from ignorance to self-knowledge, from passivity to creativity, from self-centeredness to concern for others are never purely natural events, determined by the human resources available to men; they are always co-determined by divine grace; they are always supernatural. (Gregory Baum)[11]

But I am persuaded that in the Quaker experience of Divine Presence there is a serious retention of both time and the timeless, with the final value and significance located in the Eternal, who is the creative root of time itself. For "I saw also that there was an ocean of darkness and death, but an infinite ocean of light and love which flowed over the ocean of darkness." The possibility of this experience of Divine Presence, as a repeatedly realized and present fact, and its transforming and trans-figuring effect upon all life — this is the central message of Friends. (Thomas R. Kelly)[12]

Grace is a synthesis of generosity, freedom and power. For the most high God, it is also the possibility of being not only with the lowliest, but also with the most wretched of creatures. Grace even makes God prefer what is wretched to what is sublime. (Yves Congar)[13]

Prayer

Come, Holy Spirit, come! Give us the wisdom and under-standing to see reality as you see it — in all its splendor and wretchedness. Unless we name both grace and sin, we will get stuck in ignorance and fear. And as we gaze upon sin and its effects, help us to perceive how we are sustained and surrounded by divine love. Come, Holy Spirit, come!

5. Reconciliation Draws Us into Contemplating the Mystery of the Cross Wherein We Experience the Revelation of God's Extravagant Mercy and the Depth of Our Personal and Collective Sin.

Is there any more difficult task on our Christian journey than to kneel before the cross and contemplate the suffering of Jesus? To be there with loving attention demands a courage that far exceeds our human nature. Yet it is precisely by dwelling upon the mystery of a crucified God that we come to realize how deeply God treasures us. Calvary will be forever the crossroad of human history. It is here that a redeeming God makes manifest the gracious mystery of divine creativity.

Only in the light of the cross and of that judgment on sin can the sinner gain any sort of understanding and estimate of his own sin. Even a good conscience, as it is called, in contradistinction to a bad one, does not suffice for this, necessary though it be; for the essence of sin is falsehood, a darkening of the inner sight.

(Hans Urs von Balthasar)[14]

Our work is to keep alive a deep, constant awareness of the living *love* of God; to be, as never before, contemplatives of Christ in ourselves and in one another; to keep His passion before us and to keep our faith in His love, never allowing the despair and pessimism which must sweep many hearts to shake ours.

(Caryll Houselander / Maisie Ward)[15]

The cross is the communication of God's care but it is not a message from the outside. God loves us by receiving our lives into himself as we experience them — torn and broken. The Cross is God loving us from the inside. God has accepted those aspects of our lives we ourselves have disowned and denied. We fight the awareness of our guilt, proving ourselves innocent at all costs. We fear suffering and death so fiercely that it dominates our imagination and dictates to us the shape of our lives. If Creation is God's presence to our beauty, the Cross is God's presence in our pain and twistedness.

(John Shea)[16]

Prayer

Jesus crucified, may we adore Thee as our Savior and Redeemer. Indeed, you are also our Brother and Friend, but until we taste the depth of your mercy and love we will never become mature disciples. Draw us into the mystery of your heart, a heart longing for the restoration of all creation.

6. Reconciliation Confronts Two Major Parasites: Guilt and Shame.

Sin has two offspring: guilt and shame. These results of doing wrong need to be properly honored. Admission of guilt witnesses personal honesty; feeling shame from injuring another is a sign that we are normal. The problems arise when either guilt or shame are exaggerated or denied; the problem arises when healthy responses turn neurotic. It is then that guilt and shame become parasites and eat away at our well-being. Jesus came to help us embrace our responsibility for all that we do and to set us free from those forces that make us sick and morbid. Jesus came to bring us to the fullness of life.

> Healthy guilt is appropriate — in quantity and quality — to the deed. Healthy guilt leads to remorse but not self-hate. Healthy guilt discourages us from repeating our guilty act without shutting down a wide range of our passions and pleasures. (Judith Viorst)[17]

> Real guilt should be liberating and creative; it should strive to restore things to place, to restore the good, to rejoice in the release from evil. A proper sense of guilt creates energy, restores personal relationships with man and God, gives peace. (William Lynch)[18]

> Hoping in death to find escape from shame.[19] (Dante)

Prayer

Gracious God, Lord of mercy, we do feel ashamed of our sins and guilty for not doing what you ask of us. Open our minds and hearts to an awareness of your mercy and love. Only then will our shame be healed and our guilt be expiated. We are your prodigal children; be for us, once again, a prodigal Father.

7. Reconciliation "Reconnects" Us to One Another and to God; Sin "Disconnects" Us from God and from One Another.

St. Paul's uses the analogy of grafting to illustrate how God longs to be in union with all creation. Unless the branch is connected to the vine it cannot have life, it cannot bear fruit. Reconciliation deals with separation, the disconnect that isolates us and deprives of us of the source of life. One of the major "disconnectors" or sins is that of a radical self-reliance tempting us to live autonomous lives. Just as the bird needs the air and the fish the sea, so too we need God's divine milieu in order to live and bear fruit, fruit that will last.

In a sense, this terrible situation is the pattern and prototype of all sin: the deliberate and formal will to reject disinterested love for us for the purely arbitrary reason that we simply do not want it. We will to separate ourselves from that love. (Thomas Merton)[20]

Man, separating himself from God in full consciousness of the fact, is likewise separated, by the same act, from his fellow man and from the world in which he was

placed. The separation of man from God is thus the cause of the separation of man from man and of man from nature. The result of this is to divide man in himself and to prevent him from acting in light and in freedom.
(François Roustang)[21]

In any case, sin is separation. To be in the state of sin is to be in the state of separation. And separation is threefold: there is separation among individual lives, separation of a man from himself, and separation of all men from the Ground of Being. This three-fold separation constitutes the state of everything that exists: it is a universal fact; it is the fate of every life. (Paul Tillich)[22]

Prayer

Creator God, give us the wisdom to understand our true nature. We were made for communion and community. Do not let us be separated from you or one another. Draw us into your life and love that we may then share these gifts with others. Apart from you we are incapable of doing anything.

8. Reconciliation Is an Antidote to the Poison of Unconfessed Sins.

Naming grace and naming sin are two of the most important dimensions of the spiritual life. What goes unnamed has tremendous power over us — ask any psychologist. Grace unnamed inhibits spiritual growth; sin unnamed can poison and destroy the soul. To be reconciled we must confess those attitudes and behaviors that have injured God and others. Confession sets us free because it puts us back in the land of truth. Unconfessed sins can easily become an epidemic, a spiritual influenza that destroys not only oneself but many around us.

> Not defiance but self-deception is the most fatal and widespread disease of the human heart. People live and die in sin, not because they consciously rebel against God, but because they do not know that there is anything wrong in their relation to their Maker. They are guilty of self-righteousness — the one attitude that seems to defy the grace of God — not because they put their trust in external observances, but because they cannot see any reason for trying to achieve a "righteousness" — whether that of the Pharisees, or that which exceeds it — other than the goodness they imagine themselves to possess without trying. Their eyes are blinded, their sense of need is unawakened, and they remain estranged from God and cut off from their true life. (Brigid E. Herman)[23]

Naming grace and naming sin are two of the most important dimensions of the spiritual life. What goes unnamed has tremendous power over us — ask any psychologist.

Vietnam still lurks in our national life as an unrepented sin. It is a history we do not want to face, but we must. Like any unconfessed sin, it continues to poison the body politic. (James Wallis)[24]

A clean confession, combined with a promise never to commit the sin again, when offered before one who has the right to receive it, is the purest type of repentance. I know that my confession made my father feel absolutely safe about me, and increased his affection for me beyond measure. (Mohandas Gandhi)[25]

In confession the breakthrough to community takes place. Sin demands to have a man by himself. The more isolated a person is, the more destructive will the power of sin be over him, and the more deeply he becomes involved in it, the more disastrous is his isolation. Sin wants to remain unknown. It shuns the light. In the darkness of the unexpressed it poisons the whole being of the person. (Dietrich Bonhoeffer)[26]

Prayer

Merciful Lord, we come before you repentant. We have sinned; we have done what is wrong. Have mercy on us. Take away the poison that sin spreads through our person and the community. Heal us by your merciful grace and give us the courage of honesty. We long for your forgiveness; we seek your peace.

9. Reconciliation Is the Channel of Grace's Lightness and Expansiveness; by Contrast, Sin Is Weighty and Depressing.

Sin, like depression, weighs us down. It is a yoke and burden that prevents us from enjoying the freedom of the daughters and sons of God. Grace, by contrast, brings lightness of being and a buoyancy that enables us to fly in the currents of light and love. What is at issue here is death and life, slavery and freedom, darkness and glory. Thus, our freedom is realized, once again, as a gift and a serious responsibility. We have the capacity to say yes or no to God's will.

> This special objectivity, the weight of sin, is what makes it such a burden. Sins are the heaviest burdens people carry and the greatest impediments to a simple life. They weigh us down and threaten to sink the fragile vessel of human life. Sin also ties both victim and perpetrator to the past, preventing genuine forward movement. Every future event becomes instead a replay of old scenes.
>
> (Howard Bleichner)[27]

> When we held Owen Meany above our heads, when we passed him back and forth — so effortlessly — we believed that Owen weighed nothing at all. We did not realize that there were forces beyond our play. Now I know they were the forces that contributed to our illusion of Owen's weightlessness; they were the forces we didn't have the faith to feel, they were the forces we failed to believe in — and they were also lifting up Owen Meany, taking him out of our hands. (John Irving)[28]

> It [the experience of grace] may, for example, be indescribable joy, unconditional personal love, unconditional obedience to conscience, the experience of loving union with the universe, the experience of irretrievable vulnerability of one's own human existence beyond one's own control, and so on. (Karl Rahner)[29]

> "The light comes," she [Evelyn Underhill] writes, "when it does come, rather suddenly and strangely I think. It is just like falling in love; a thing that never happens to those who are always trying to do it." (Dana Greene)[30]

Prayer

Father of the prodigal son, relieve us of the burden of sin. Remove the yoke that crushes our fragile spirit; set us free to once again be your beloved creatures. Without your mercy we live in fear and dread; without your love we are overwhelmed by the burdens we inflict upon ourselves. Come, merciful God, and grant us forgiveness and peace.

10. Reconciliation Is the Story of God's Healing Presence in Human History.

The three chapters in the original "divine comedy" are creation, redemption, and the gift of the Holy Spirit. Our Creator God began the story by giving us life; in Jesus, the eternal Son, God enters into the brokenness of human history and misery and reconciles us to the Father; through the gift of the Holy Spirit, God's peace, we are now empowered to continue the story, to continue the mission and ministry of Jesus. Reconciliation is the story of Jesus, our Savior, our Friend, our Redeemer. We cannot afford to forget the story; we must tell the story to our children and our children's children lest we lose all sense of meaning.

There is a moment in every great story in which the presence of grace can be felt as it waits to be accepted or rejected, even though the reader may not recognize this moment. (Flannery O'Connor)[31]

The man who truly helps others is close to God. He is very close to that saving God who embraces us in our exile, who receives the beggar, who pulls the drowning toward himself, who is the God of all the broken, outlawed and lost; the God who blesses even our misfortunes; who descended into the terrible depths of the human soul and faced the dark shadow of death for our sakes; the God of those who are given over to loneliness, the God who tenderly loves the least of us and the most hopeless; the God of unembittered yet supplicating love.

(Ladislas Boros)[32]

I have seen God take the broken, deformed things of this world, bless them with new life and sanctify them for his special purpose. From a broken tree, God provides shade in the summer. From a deeply scarred youth, he forms a person of unusual compassion and understanding, a model of hope to the disheartened of the inner city. From the twisted personality of a counselor, he shapes a healer of emotional pain and uses a rebellious nature for creative purposes.

I am reassured to know that the straightness of my grain is not a precondition of usefulness to God. And I am humbled to see that out of the twistedness of my wounds, he designs for me a special place of service.

(Robert D. Lupton)[33]

Prayer

Jesus, continue to tell your story through our lives. May we be lifegiving, healing agents, and instruments of your peace. Your story is a love story: creative, redemptive, and transforming. Help us not to forget our lines or our supportive roles. Give us the grace of hope so that our story does not end like a Shakespearean tragedy, but like it truly is, a divine, loving comedy.

Chapter Six

Sacrament of Reconciliation

THE FORMULA of absolution for the sacrament of reconciliation deserves our prayerful reflection:

> God, the Father of mercies,
> through the death and the resurrection of his Son
> has reconciled the world to himself
> and sent the Holy Spirit among us
> for the forgiveness of sins;
> through the ministry of the Church
> may God give you pardon and peace,
> and I absolve you from your sins
> in the name of the Father, and of the Son,
> and of the Holy Spirit.

Our God, revealed in Jesus, is a God of mercy and love. If
our concept of God is ill-formed or immature we will have a
difficult time approaching this powerful sacrament. If God is
conceived as a harsh judge who has a massive tome recording
all of our crimes and misdemeanors, then fear and anxiety will
dominate our disposition. The God revealed through Jesus
is a God of mercy, who compassionately understands our
temptations, failures, and sins.

In this prayer of absolution we are given a Triune God: a Father of mercies; Jesus, God's Son, who is our redeemer and who restores all things; and, the Holy Spirit, who forgives our sins and who gives us the gift of peace. Thus we have in this prayer the great mysteries of our faith: the Trinity and the Incarnation. Our tradition is rich in its theological language, which attempts to put into words, inadequate as they are, our faith understanding of God. So, in regard to the Trinity, we have such categories as Father, Son, and Spirit; Creator, Redeemer, and Sanctifier; Light, Love, Life; Lover, Beloved, Loving. This attempt to name the Trinity is of great importance since we, who are made in the image and likeness of God, come to a greater self-knowledge to the extent that we understand the mystery of God.

The Incarnation is the mystery of our redemption. Jesus came to proclaim the Kingdom, to give us the fullness of life, to reconcile the world to himself. Jesus continues his saving work through the sacraments. Our fragile lives and bent world constantly need healing. Jesus continues his saving work by healing through the gift of the Holy Spirit.

The prayer of absolution clearly shows that the church has been given the ministry of continuing the mission of Jesus. Our holy and sinful faith community is to be sign and instrument of union with God and unity among all peoples. Thus, the sacrament of reconciliation is an ecclesial reality. God's grace is mediated through human instruments. Two things are offered to those who confess their sins with humility and earnestness: pardon and peace. These incredible graces restore us to friendship with God and the community. To be pardoned liberates us from shame and guilt; to be given peace, puts us back in good relationships.

Examination of Conscience:
Fruits of the Holy Spirit

It is important that we assess our lives in the light of God's word. Turning to St. Paul's letter to the Galatians, we are given a list of the fruits of the Holy Spirit. St. Paul writes: "Now the works of the flesh are obvious: fornication, impurity, licentiousness, idolatry, sorcery, enmities, strife, jealousy, anger, quarrels, dissensions, factions, envy, drunkenness, carousing, and things like these. I am warning you, as I warned you before: those who do such things will not inherit the Kingdom of God. By contrast, the fruits of the Spirit are love, joy, peace, patience, kindness, generosity, faithfulness, gentleness, and self-control. There is no law against such things" (Gal. 5:19–23). These nine qualities provide an excellent framework as we review our lives from a Christian perspective.

Love

Time and time again we are drawn back to the bedrock of our Christian life: to be loved and to love. Not to receive and transmit love is to miss the meaning of life. And this love is not some romantic emotion or feeling. Rather, it is a solid love that is sacrificial, enduring, and powerful. It involves such qualities as deep respect for every person, an active concern for the well-being of others, and an acceptance of responsibility for one another. Love is grounded in knowledge. We cannot love God, others, or ourselves without some awareness of who they (we) are and what they (we) do. This means that communication will play a major role in our ability to be loved and to love.

Evelyn Underhill, the Anglican spiritual writer, once commented: "To be unloving is to be out of touch with God."

Sin is being out of touch with God. As we look into our lives we must ask: Am I really concerned about the well-being of others? Do I respect and reverence everyone I meet? Do I fulfill my obligations with joy? How deeply do I know God and others? Is my love conditional — I will love you if...? Do I ask for the grace of love on a daily basis?

Holiness is essentially the perfection of love. Our common vocation is the call to holiness. Because of our innate weaknesses and limitations, we need to turn to the Spirit of the Father and Jesus and ask the Holy Spirit to love through us. It is primarily through the work of the Spirit that we participate in that loving life.

Joy

Someone once said that joy is the infallible sign of God's presence. Joy is an experiential awareness that God has given us good things such as life, love, freedom, family, and friends. To recognize how blessed we are and to acknowledge the source of these blessings is to grow in joy. Obviously, we are talking about happiness, a deep delight in life. Yet there is so much sadness and depression in our world. This melancholy lies in an awareness of the negative forces that impinge on the human spirit: violence, hatred, poverty, illness, death — yes, sin! Doing even the briefest social analysis can bring depression.

The French spiritual writer François Roustang maintained: "Joy leads us to supreme activity." By contrast, sadness causes inertia. We imitate our God by being joyful, for God takes delight in his creative activity. As we know from Genesis, God saw that what he had created was good, indeed, very good. So are we a joyful people? Do we delight in all the good things that are part of our existence? Do we rejoice in the achievement of others and take delight in their accomplishments? Are we perpetually sad and downcast, focusing on the negative forces of life? Do we smile? Do we laugh? Do we express our joy through humor and good stories? Are we made for joy?

The story of the pregnant Mary visiting the pregnant Elizabeth is a story of joy. The infant John stirred for joy in the womb of Elizabeth as Mary and the child in her womb came to visit. That is what joy is all about: stirring into new life. When love is present, joy is just around the corner. The church has sung for two thousand years Mary's hymn: "My soul magnifies the Lord, and my spirit rejoices in God my Savior" (Luke 1:46–47). Why? Because God's creative, joyful, creative love had done great things for Mary and, indeed, for us.

Peace

Is there any greater gift than peace? In the prayer of absolution two graces are given to us penitents: pardon and peace. When Jesus appeared to the disciples after his resurrection — disciples who had sinned by denial, betrayal, and cowardice — the message was always the same: "Peace be with you." Jesus' love was unconditional and the byproduct of that love is peace. And when that peace was appropriated on Pentecost through the power of the Spirit, fear vanished and courage was restored. The disciples ventured forth to continue the ministry of reconciliation by passing on the pardon and peace they had received.

The Asian Archbishop Fumio Hamao wrote: "Peace is the final gift, the result of a harmonious and mature integration of fairness, justice, love, truth, liberty, and respect for all."[1] So, we might ask ourselves: Are we at peace? Do I deal fairly with others? What is the quality of my justice? Do I protect and promote the rights of others? Am I truly free or do I deal with various addictions such as alcohol, smoking, or eating disorders? Are there any relationships that need mending or tending? As we examine our conscience, we must realize that peace is ultimately a gift and it is there for the asking. We dispose ourselves to receiving this gift by confessing our sins.

Gerard Manley Hopkins, the great religious poet, maintained that "piecemeal peace is poor peace." Who can argue with that? On this pilgrim journey our peace will never be entirely whole. Yet we are a people of hope and we live with the conviction that the peace of Christ is offered time and time again. As we journey toward God's Kingdom, we participate in that glorious process of receiving God's peace and passing it on to others. Indeed, may the Lord make us an instrument of his peace.

Patience

Waiting is a difficult art for us humans. Immediate gratification appears to be the ideal. Yet, aware of the human condition and the necessity of growth, we are challenged to embrace our situation and make the most of it. God is patient with us, giving us year after year to respond to the divine initiative. We, too, are to be patient with one another with a compassion that appreciates our different personalities and unique circumstances. We must constantly fight the temptation to hurry and thereby desecrate time. All things have their season; ripeness may, indeed, be almost everything.

In her classic *Gift from the Sea,* Anne Morrow Lindbergh writes:

The sea does not reward those who are too anxious, too greedy, or too impatient. To dig for treasures shows not only impatience and greed, but lack of faith. Patience, patience, patience, is what the sea teaches. Patience and faith. One should lie empty, open, choiceless as a beach — waiting for a gift from the sea.[2]

So we might ask: Am I able to wait for others to grow up as well as myself? Are my expectations of God and life realistic or neurotic? Do I honor time and its gracious tempo? In what ways do I seek immediate gratification? What is my external and internal response when I don't get my way? In what ways do greed and anxiety cause me to be impatient? How deep is my faith and trust in God's providence?

"We wait, but lack the wisdom of them that wait," writes Brigid E. Herman.[3] Patience is a grace and its underside is wisdom. Waiting has the capacity to create an emptiness that must not be too quickly filled. God is looking for room, and when we wait on the Lord, not filling our waiting with entertainment, food, and frenetic activity, we have the possibility of experiencing a divine visitation. Wisdom is to know when to remain in patient solitude and when to exert every ounce of energy to achieve what God wants us to do *now*.

Kindness

In Shakespeare's *The Merchant of Venice*, Portia is walking in the night and spots a candle in a distant window. She reflects: " . . . so shines a good deed in a naughty world." Our world is naughty, indeed, often quite mean. Torture and cruelty are not sporadic happenings. On a lesser scale, but nonetheless important, is a basic meanness that is expressed in ignoring another person, putting people down in public, being a bully.

Our dark world needs random acts of kindness. Opening a door for another, sending a note of affirmation, giving someone a pat on the back are all ways in which the light of grace begins to illumine our world.

George Herbert got it right: " . . . All worldly joys go less / To the one joy of doing kindnesses." Here we begin to see an overlap among the fruits of the Holy Spirit. Being kind brings joy; loving others fosters peace; patience expresses self-control. As we approach the sacrament of reconciliation and reflect upon the kindnesses or lack thereof in our life, we might ask: Do I have a mean streak in my heart that needs careful watching? Have I expressed gratitude to those who have been kind to me? Is the language I use kind, filled with words that are positive and affirming? What lights of kindness have I brought to a naughty, dark world? What was the greatest act of kindness I did? And, what was the greatest act of meanness? Am I kind to myself?

Robert Louis Stevenson wrote, "It is the history of our kindnesses that alone makes this world tolerable. If it were not for that, the effects of kind words, kind looks, kind letters . . . I should be inclined to think our life a practical jest in the worst possible spirit."[4] The daily newspaper will report on the motorists who stop to help someone with a flat tire, or the neighbor who sent over food to a poor family, or the volunteer who sat with a stranger who was dying. Yet, are not these the moments of grace that fill our lives with rich meaning and give us hope? And the more anonymous the better. Kind looks, kind letters, kind gifts, kind words, kind visitations! Maybe, just maybe, the world and all of us will be less naughty. In the movie *Pay It Forward* about a boy, Trevor, we see someone who made the world better by doing good deeds and convincing others to do the same.

Generosity

The psalmist cries out: "What shall I return to the Lord for all his bounty to me?" (Ps. 116:12). We are here in the land of stewardship, the land where we recognize that everything we are and have is gift. The basic fact is that we are poor, indeed, radically indigent. Once we get in touch with this reality and are existentially aware of our emptiness — yet filled with so many blessings — then gratitude begins to overflow into a life of generosity. The steward is one who gives away freely the time, talent, and treasure that has come one's way.

But this picture does not correspond with history. So often we think that gifts originate with us, or that they are due to us, or perhaps we simply take them for granted. This is my time; these are my talents; this is my money. We live the lie and then wonder why there is "something" wrong with our lives. So, we might ask: Do I return to the Lord a substantial portion of my time, talent, and treasure? Do I take things for granted, even become demanding in regard to the goods of this earth? Am I a member of the culture of complaint or the Kingdom of God? How many hours of the week do I give to reading the newspaper, watching TV? How many hours do I give to prayer? What talents and gifts do I share for the sake of the common good? What percent of my annual income do I give to the church and charities?

In Flannery O'Connor's short story "Greenleaf" we read: "Some people learn gratitude too late, Mr. Greenleaf, and some never learn it at all." One hears in this statement St. Augustine's famous "Too late have I loved Thee, O Lord, too late have I loved Thee." Not to experience gratitude and not to express that gratitude in generosity is a great tragedy in life. More, it is to miss out on the meaning of life, which is the reception and transmission of God's light, love, and life. Through the sacrament of reconciliation we kneel before the Lord confessing our lack of gratitude and praying for the grace of generosity.

Faithfulness

Spirituality is about relationship. God has entered into a covenant with us and invites us into a life of friendship. Are we faithful to this precious grace? Fidelity implies, as we know from the marriage commitment, that one remains true to the other in good times and in bad, in illness and good health, in rain or sunshine — unto death. Few of us can claim perfect fidelity. It is not that there is some massive betrayal, à la Judas, but there are small, but not insignificant, breakdowns in our promises to God and others. Failure to communicate, withholding of affirmation or affection, basic neglect, might show up on our list. Thus, the need for forgiveness and ongoing reconciliation.

In preparing for the sacrament, a series of questions seem appropriate: Have I been faithful to God through personal prayer and public worship? Do I assume responsibility for building the Kingdom by being an agent of truth and charity? In my personal relationships, am I intellectually and emotionally honest? Do I keep my promises? Am I clear about expectations? Have I endangered the fidelity of others by inappropriate speech or action? Do I support others and help them keep their commitment by sound advice and good example?

Willa Cather, in her tender novel *My Antonia,* writes: "These two fellows had been faithful to us through sun and storm, had given us things that cannot be bought in any market in the world." No monetary value can be assigned to the grace of fidelity and commitment. To know that someone is there, "through sun and storm," is a rich consolation. And to be an instrument of such a grace, to be there for others whatever the season, bring incredible peace. Our God is a faithful God. When we stray from the path of commitment, God is there to touch our conscience and lead us home. Surely, the prodigal son sensed his infidelity as if it were a raw nerve. He faced his sin and sought forgiveness. We can do no better.

Gentleness

Things and people break easily. We must be tender and gentle if we are to live the Christian life. This is in no way softness; rather, only the strong can afford to be gentle. Jesus instructs his disciples to be "meek and gentle of heart" if they are to fulfill their commitment as disciples. This gentleness verges on compassion, a deep sensitivity to the plight of others. Everyone is struggling — everyone, without exception. What a grace it is to encounter a gentle soul on the pilgrimage and to be enriched with a soft glance and a kind word.

Looking into our souls we might ask: Am I gentle with myself? What is my tone of voice in addressing others? Am I aware of the wounds and fragility of those around me? Do I have "soft" eyes and a tender voice? What is my understanding of Jesus' invitation to a meek and gentle heart? Is my image of God one of gentleness? Can I be accused of hardness of heart?

St. Francis de Sales, a doctor of the church, has some wise advice:

Don't lose any opportunity, however small, of being gentle toward everyone. Don't rely in your own efforts to succeed in your various undertakings, but only on

God's help. Then rest in His care of you, confident that He will do what is best for you, provided that you, for your part, work diligently but gently. I say "gently" because a tense diligence is harmful both to our heart and to our task and is not really diligence, but overeagerness and anxiety.[5]

> *Things and people break easily. We must be tender and gentle if we are to live the Christian life. This is in no way softness; rather, only the strong can afford to be gentle.*

In our pragmatic, "seven-habits-of-highly-effective-leaders" culture, we have an innate tendency to think that we are in charge of every dimension of our life. Especially in this area of gentleness, we must realize the importance of God's help in avoiding that overeagerness and tense diligence that throws the heart into chaos. It's not unlike the golfer who grips the golf club so hard that the body cannot do its work. The great golfer has a "gentle" swing and an easy tempo that makes the game look simple. So too we must relax and let God be God in directing our spiritual life.

Self-Control

St. Paul's ninth sign of the Holy Spirit is self-control. Without a basic discipline, our lives lose focus and become dissipated. Sensual, moral, and intellectual desires must be held in check lest the order that brings peace be forfeited. Given that we live in a culture of self-indulgence, we do not have the societal supports of the self-control essential to a life of discipleship. Much grace is needed here. We need mentors and models who will point the way. Perhaps we could learn a warning and metaphorical lesson from the man who gorged himself in Monty Python's *The Meaning of Life*.

As we celebrate reconciliation we do well to ask: Are there any areas of my life that are out of control? What is my response to the Lord's injunction about fasting? Do I ask for the grace to control my imagination and my language? In what areas of my life am I self-indulgent: food? drink? inappropriate sexuality? Do I have to deal with addictions in entertainment or gambling? How does my lack of self-control impact on the lives of others? In what specific area of my life is the Lord asking me to exercise more discipline?

Self-discipline has many effects. In his book *Reason and Emotion*, John MacMurray states: "Its [discipline's] achievement is shown in the freedom and grace of action; in its rhythmic quality; in the absence of jerkiness and effort" (84). There is yet another side effect of self-control: joy. Jesus insisted on prayer, fasting, and giving alms. All three of these spiritual activities involve a high degree of discipline. And we can be assured that when the Lord asks, he gives us grace to live these commands.

Examination of Conscience: Theological and Moral Virtues

Another approach in reviewing our life in Christ is to take the theological and moral virtues and examine our conscience in light of them. The theological virtues — faith, hope, and charity — establish a deep relationship with God. The moral virtues — prudence, justice, fortitude, and temperance — address our relationship to one another and our self. Here is a brief litany that might help us get in touch with our need for forgiveness when we have failed to live a virtuous life.

Lord Jesus, you call us to faith and trust. For the times we have failed to believe in you and your word; for the times that we have entertained doubts and failed to trust in your loving providence, we pray: Lord, have mercy.

Lord Jesus, you call us to be hopeful and joyful. For the times we have allowed discouragement, even despair, to block our hope in the future; for the times we procrastinated and let a sense of futility dominate our days, we pray: Lord, have mercy.

Lord Jesus, you call us to be loved and to love. For the times we have not reached out to those in need; for the times we have withheld proper affections and affirmation; for the times we have not passed on your love to others, we pray: Lord, have mercy.

Lord Jesus, you call us to be prudent — to deliberate, to judge, and to act. For the times we have failed to put into action our knowledge of the good; for the times we have not discerned your will and acted rashly; for the times we have failed to be decisive, we pray: Lord, have mercy.

Lord Jesus, you call us to be a just people. For the times we have not protected or promoted the rights of others, especially the most vulnerable; for the times we have not fulfilled our duties and obligations; for the times we have not been prophetic in addressing major moral issues, we pray: Lord, have mercy.

Lord Jesus, you call us to courage and fortitude. For the times we have been cowards in facing suffering and death; for the times we have not endured the crosses that you ask us to carry; for the times we have let fear dominate our hearts, we pray: Lord, have mercy.

Lord Jesus, you call us to moderation and temperance. For the times we have not used food, drink, and human sexuality in accordance with your plans; for the times we have been self-indulgent and gluttonous; for the times we took much more than we needed, we pray: Lord, have mercy.

Conclusion

"God, the Father of mercies," these are words that remind us that as we deal with the reality of sin in our lives we must be careful to keep a clear focus. It is extremely dangerous to look at our sins and what those sins do apart from the gaze of God's mercy. As we draw this chapter on the examination of our conscience to a conclusion, a poem by Jessica Powers might help us make sure that the sacrament is more about God's mercy than it is about our sinfulness. Listen attentively to what the poet says about God's grace-filled wardrobe:

THE GARMENTS OF GOD

God sits on a chair of darkness in my soul.
He is God alone, supreme in His majesty.
I sit at His feet, a child in the dark beside Him;
my joy is aware of His glance and my sorrow is tempted
to nest on the thought that His face is turned from me.

He is clothed in the robes of His mercy, voluminous
    garments —
not velvet or silk and affable to the touch,
but fabric strong for a frantic hand to clutch,
and I hold to it fast with the fingers of my will.
Here is my cry of faith, my deep avowal
to the Divinity that I am dust.
Here is the loud profession of my trust.
I need not go abroad
to the hills of speech or the hinterlands of music
for a crier to walk in my soul where all is still.
I have this potent prayer through good or ill:
here in the dark I clutch the garments of God.[6]

Questions and Answers

Question: *What is the ordinary way of celebrating the sacrament of reconciliation? Are there other forms besides the ordinary way?*

Answer: The sacrament of reconciliation begins with a greeting and blessing by the priest. Then a brief passage from God's word is read to dispose the penitent to see more clearly the nature of sin and to experience God's mercy. The penitent then confesses his or her sins and makes an act of contrition. There may then be a brief dialogue between the priest and penitent if this seems appropriate and helpful. Then the priest assigns a penance that may take the form of an action or the saying of some prayers. Absolution is then given, followed by a word of dismissal and blessing.

In most cases, the penitent has an option of celebrating the sacrament face to face or behind a screen. The option is important so that anonymity might be maintained if so desired. The face-to-face format can be much more personal and meaningful for some.

There are two other ways of celebrating this sacrament. One is a communal form in which a number of people gather for the sacrament. The liturgy often begins with a song, a greeting, and prayer by the priest. Then God's word is proclaimed, followed by a reflection and examination of conscience. A communal request for forgiveness can also be made. Then each individual has the opportunity to confess his or her sins to the priest and to receive a penance and absolution. Often the community then says together the Our Father and prayer of thanksgiving. The format allows considerable variation.

A third form of celebration is a communal celebration that involves a general confession and a general absolution. Only in case of grave necessity is this form permitted. This could be in a situation where there is imminent danger of death such as warfare or where time is not available for individual confession. Also, grave necessity could arise when there is a shortage of priests and a large community has gathered, making it impossible within a reasonable period of time to hear all the confessions. Another condition in this circumstance is that penitents would be deprived of the grace of the sacrament or the Eucharist for a long length of time, through no fault of their own. Each diocesan bishop determines the conditions necessary for general absolution.

Q.: *Why do we confess the number and kinds of sins rather than some general disclosure of faults and weaknesses?*

A.: There is an old adage that power lies in the details. Another way of saying this is that vagueness, generalities, weak specification are great dangers to the spiritual life. Details and specifics help us to get in touch with our faith journey. If I were to say, "One of these days I am going to begin to pray," probably nothing will happen. But if we specify time and place, we are serious about the spiritual journey: "On Monday, Wednesday, and Friday, at seven o'clock each morning, I am going to spend fifteen minutes reading and reflecting upon the Bible." Now we are in business.

So too with the sacrament of reconciliation. It is one thing to "confess": "I wasn't very good these past several months," or, "My attitude was somewhat negative during the season of Lent," or "I did not use God's gift of language in the proper way." These general, abstract, and nebulous statements reveal little about one's spiritual condition. How much different if I were to confess: "on four separate occasions I hurt my spouse's feelings by deliberately speeding just to get her upset," or that "three times I thought ill of others simply because they were of a different ethnic background," or that "four times I fudged on the truth leaving other people confused or ignorant on important business deals that had major consequences."

By being specific and concrete, we are dealing seriously and honestly with our relationship with God and with one another. When we confess in this way, both shame and guilt no longer have power over us.

Q.: *Why must one confess one's sins to a priest? Can't a person simply confess to God?*

A.: Within the Catholic tradition, we believe in the principle of sacramentality. This means that God has chosen to offer us love, light, and life through various channels and instruments. Grace is mediated, that is, given to us through persons, signs, and symbols. Because we are incarnate beings, people with a body and soul, God comes to us in our human circumstances. Thus, through the sacrament of reconciliation a priest is the one who mediates God's grace and we, the recipients of that grace, hear words of absolution and are given a penance to help us grow in God's life.

A second reason why we confess to a priest and do not simply go to God alone is that we are members of a community. Sin not only offends God; it disrupts our community.

Even in the most private of sins, because we have turned from God, we are less for others. Whatever the sin, private or public, it diminishes our dignity. Be that sin interior envy or public jealousy, private thoughts of revenge or public acts of violence, the individual and the communities are injured. The priest represents God and the community. By going to confession, we reconnect with the Body of Christ.

A third reason for confession is that specifically naming our sins and telling them to another human person, gives us knowledge and a fuller sense of reality. Things not spoken or written can remain "half real." But when we use words to describe what or who we are, greater growth can happen, freeing us from a vague and undefined interior world.

Through the forgiveness of sin we are put back into right relationship with God and with one another.

A fourth reason why we confess to a priest is so we can receive an objective look at our lives. Self-knowledge is a tricky business. Just as we need a mirror to see how we look, we need others to know ourselves. They can reflect back to us our initial self-awareness and name our attitudes or behaviors for which we do not have words. The fields of psychology and psychiatry demonstrate how helpful and important it is to have a listening ear.

A fifth factor is that being given a penance enhances the chance of reformation and transformation. We are called to conversion, to turn from darkness to light, from death to life, from indifference to love. Given concrete acts to do increases the probability that we will change our lifestyle. Left alone most of us wallow in a sea of nebulous resolutions.

A sixth factor is that confession brings closure. We need someone to tell us, as Jesus told many sinners in so many words: Enough. Stop torturing yourself. God loves you. You are forgiven. Sin no more. Go in the love of Christ to serve others. Because sin is an offense against God and community, we need the peace that their forgiveness — through the priest — brings.

Q.: *Am I not forgiven just as soon as I am sorry for my sins?*

A.: God's forgiveness and mercy come in many ways and according to God's own timing. Within our Catholic tradition, contrition and sorrow are essential elements in our understanding of forgiveness. But we also hold that in the case of serious sin two other elements are necessary: confession and satisfaction or penance. Obviously, when a person does not have recourse to the sacrament because of circumstances, forgiveness can be experienced by God's grace. But when the sacrament is available and serious sin is the issue, confession and penance are necessary.

Q.: *What are the essential elements of the sacrament of reconciliation?*

A.: There are three essential acts of the penitent: contrition, confession, and satisfaction. Contrition means that one is truly sorrow for having offended God and others in word, deed, or neglect. Part of that contrition is a firm resolve not to sin again. Confession means disclosing one's sins. By this act a person takes full responsibility for his or her behavior and willingly faces the guilt caused by sin. This demands both honesty and humility. Satisfaction deals with the disorder and harm done by sin. This satisfaction, sometimes known as penance, involves some concrete way of re-establishing justice and repairing the harm done by sin.

In Shakespeare's *Romeo and Juliet* we read: "Could we but learn from whence his sorrows grow, / We would as willingly give cure as know."[1] We do know, deep inside, from whence our sorrows come. They come from sin; they come from hurting one another and offending our God. A "perfect act" of contrition lies in a deep and firm commitment to avoid all sin. Given our human condition, however, we know that as long as we are on the pilgrim journey, contrition will be a recurring event.

The second essential element for the sacrament is confession. We indicate to the confessor the number and kinds of sins for which we are sorry. This moment of personal revelation has powerful consequences: a new freedom, in that truth does set us free; a deeper authenticity from claiming the dark side of life as truly our own; and a re-establishing of our membership in the community. The act of confessing often demands great courage, for sin brings upon us much shame.

Satisfaction or penance involves the attempt to set things right, indeed, to foster the righteousness that Jesus came to bring to all of us. This penance may be making restitution for having taken what is not ours, or going to someone we have hurt and asking forgiveness, or committing ourselves to helping the poor whom we have neglected by our sin.

Q.: *What is the ultimate purpose of the sacrament of reconciliation?*

A. The mission of Jesus was to redeem the world. He came that we might have fullness of life, which means that one day we might be with him in eternity. Thus, the purpose of the sacrament of reconciliation is to foster that union and unity that Jesus came to accomplish. Sin separates; grace unites. Through the forgiveness of sin we are put back into right relationship with God and with one another.

This means that the sacrament is about conversion, a turning away from darkness to light, from death to life, from hatred to love. It is a moral conversion in that our behavior is transformed. It is also a deep intellectual and psychological conversion wherein truth now governs our life. Thus we need brutal honesty in facing the dark side of our life. We also need to change our inner psychological disposition that can so easily alienate us from one another. Hostility must give way to hospitality; arrogance, to humility.

When the purpose of the sacrament is achieved, that is, union and unity, then we come to know that peace that St. Paul tells us is beyond our understanding. In the resurrection stories we hear time and time again: "Peace be with you." Jesus, the risen Lord, assures the frightened disciples that they are forgiven and have nothing to fear. The celebration of the sacrament ends with that same expression: "Go now in peace." And, let it be added, where there is authentic peace there will also be a deep joy. And it is a joy that might break out into song: "How can we keep from singing?"

Q.: *What are "effects" of the sacrament of reconciliation? What does the sacrament "do"?*

A.: Sin fractures our relationship with God, a relationship that is called friendship. The sacrament restores and repairs that relationship through the forgiveness of Jesus. The friendship is renewed and made whole. Two byproducts are often experienced: a deep peace and profound joy. If St. Thomas Aquinas is correct in describing grace as friendship with God, then the sacramental grace of reconciliation brings us back into union with our Triune God. And joy and peace are essential ingredients in any friendship.

Sin fractures the community in that our disobedience to God's plan alienates us from our sisters and brothers. Be it lying or murder, infidelity or neglect, people are hurt and the union that Christ desired is thwarted. The sacrament heals and restores the sinner with the community. And, like a nautical rope that is broken and mended, the final product can be stronger than the original. Thus, sinners are often stronger after receiving sacramental absolution than before they sinned and received the sacrament.

The effect of reconciliation is not limited to God and the community. A further restoration takes place deep within the sinner as personal integrity is experienced through God's grace. Further, the sinner is also reconnected with all creation, with all of life, through the power of Jesus' sacrifice and the gift of reconciliation.

The woman caught in adultery (John 8:1–11) received the forgiveness of Jesus. Through his absolution, the woman was now back in friendship with God. More, she was restored to the community as her accusers slipped away one by one as they confronted their own sinfulness and judgmental way of life. What peace and sense of wholeness must have swept through the woman's heart as this "Teacher" looked at her with compassion and love. Indeed, now things were right with the world as she felt Jesus' presence with the mandate to sin no more. Her story is all of our stories for none of us is free from sin. Jesus' words must never be forgotten: "Let anyone among you who is without sin be the first to throw a stone at her" (John 8:7b).

Q.: *How often should one celebrate the sacrament of reconciliation?*

A.: For some individuals, a monthly confession helps foster a sensitivity to God's grace and human sin. Prayerfully reflecting upon one's relationships and naming the attitudes and behaviors that diminish the quality of those relationships is a meaningful spiritual exercise. For others, bi-monthly or quarterly confession will be a routine that keeps them in touch with God's mercy. Still others make it a practice of celebrating the sacrament during Lent and Advent. Much depends upon one's self-awareness in light of God's daily call and on the sensitivity of one's conscience.

The sacrament heals and restores the sinner with the community. And, like a nautical rope that is broken and mended, the final product can be stronger than the original.

If a person is aware of a significant rupture in a relationship, the sacrament should not be postponed. A golfing analogy seems appropriate. When divots are made on the green, repairing it immediately means the green will heal within a day or two. If that divot is not fixed, healing may take weeks. Or, as the adage goes, a stitch in time saves nine. Addressing one's sin immediately is wise counsel.

Discipline is an absolute requirement in the spiritual life. That is true of prayer, acts of charity, and the celebration of the sacraments. Once patterns are broken, it is so easy to slip into non-practice, that is, non-discipline. Daily prayer is dropped, neighbors' needs are untended, Sunday Mass becomes an occasional event, and the sacrament of reconciliation is postponed for one, five, twenty years. Discipline means that we are serious about a commitment, be it physical exercise, intellectual study, or religious growth. The discipline of going to confession every month or several times a year will bring the grace of peace and joy.

Q.: *What about temptations? What are temptations and how do they influence our lives?*

A.: A classic work dealing with temptation is *The Screwtape Letters,* authored by C. S. Lewis. In a masterful, humorous, but incisive manner, Lewis has a senior devil (Screwtape) write letters to his inexperienced and junior nephew (Wormwood) regarding the best ways to tempt human beings. Screwtape writes this to Wormwood about the junior devil's client: "His increasing reputation, his widening circle of acquaintances, his sense of importance, the growing pressure of absorbing and agreeable work, build up in him a sense of being really at home on Earth, which is just what we want."[2] C. S. Lewis has a deep understanding of both human psychology and the nature of the spiritual life. Although disturbing at times, *The Screwtape Letters* should be read by anyone interested in understanding the nature of temptation and sin.

Another theologian, Fr. Karl Rahner, S.J., describes temptation in these terms: "It attacks man unexpectedly, it has in man himself an ally, his hunger for good fortune, his sadness and the melancholy of life that lusts for an anesthetic, his trust in the concrete, his mistrust of the future hereafter, his amazing and uncanny facility for moral counterfeiting which can make good evil and evil good."[3]

Jesus himself had to deal with temptations. The Scriptures record how Jesus was driven into the desert, where he had to struggle with alternative choices that were not in accord with his Father's will. Would Jesus yield to the temptations of possessions, power, and prestige? Or would Jesus refuse any form of idolatry? This was not play-acting. Jesus struggled violently with the forces that would draw him away from his destiny. We must never minimize the intensity of this interior warfare.

All of us have to contend with the desire to dominate (power), with the hunger to acquire (possessions) and with the thirst for recognition (prestige). There is a fourth "P" as well: the temptation to a life of pleasure. Conventional wisdom rejects all forms of self-denial or voluntary suffering (mortification). It is no surprise that *The Screwtape Letters* touched a nerve in describing how we are so vulnerable to a way of life that is self-centered.

Let it be noted that power and prestige, pleasure and possessions are not evils and therefore need not be rejected. Rather, they are goods, but limited goods. The trouble arises when these means become ends. Power used to bring about the common good can easily turn into an obsession of domination and control; prestige gained as president or general or pope can lead to an unhealthy elitism; the pleasure of a glass of wine or good meal can become a passion for a life of comfort. The trouble is precisely that of idolatry. Thus we need God's Spirit, the same Spirit who was with Jesus in the desert, if we are to withstand the temptations of our times. We need the Holy Spirit to say "yes" to whatever God asks of us.

In his excellent work *What Is the Point of Being a Christian?* Fr. Timothy Radcliffe has a slightly different take on the idols and temptations of our time. He writes: "Three such idols are the cultivation of limitless desire, the absolutization of private property, and the deification of money. There is nothing wrong with desire, private property, or money: they are all genuine goods. But if they are erected as absolute goods, as in our society, then they become idols, whose worship is destructive of human family, a terrible tritheistic anti-religion."[4]

Q.: *What is the relationship between the sacrament of reconciliation and both spiritual direction and psychological counseling?*

A.: Spiritual direction has to do with growth in the spiritual life. Individuals who participate in spiritual direction talk over not only the areas in their life that need forgiveness, that is, areas of sin, but even more so areas of their lives that involve physical, emotional, intellectual, and spiritual components. Many spiritual directors are not ordained priests, and thus the sacrament of reconciliation has to be celebrated with someone other than the director.

Psychological counseling deals with the problem areas of one's life. For some, it may be an addiction or family dysfunction or a basic lack of maturity. The professional counselor attempts to bring understanding to the motive for behavior as well as some behavioral change. While spirituality is not excluded automatically from counseling sessions, most psychologists are not trained in the spiritual domain and thus do not deal explicitly with the client's relationship with God and how that relationship impacts one's life.

Spiritual directors and professional counselors have a body of knowledge and a set of skills that many confessors lack. The ministries of direction and counseling are distinct from the ministry of the sacrament of reconciliation, though there will often be some overlapping. The confessor may well give some direction for spiritual growth; the confessor may offer suggestions to deal with an emotional problem or make a referral for professional help. It is important for the confessor to know his limits.

Let it be added that when sin is the main issue in a person's life, spiritual directors and counselors do well to refer their client to the sacrament, assuming here a certain degree of faith. By putting the client in the path of God's mercy, major breakthroughs can happen.

Chapter Eight ─────────────────────────────

Reconciliation:
A Poetic Perspective

INFORMATION IS IMPORTANT because it exposes us to the truth. Transformation is even more significant because it shapes our days and our destiny. Gratitude to those who inform us is well deserved; gratitude to those who radically alter our lives has eternal ramifications.

Music, art, and literature have the power not only to inform us about God, the world, and ourselves but they also carry a mysterious power to transform us and to help us realize our potential. How this happens has never been definitively described. That it happens is beyond doubt. One specific area we might focus on is power and the power of metaphor and image to influence our attitudes and shape our behavior. Here are a number of poems dealing with sin, forgiveness, reconciliation, and peace that might begin the work of transformation in our personal and collective lives. Jesus used the poetic dimension of parables to communicate his vision of the Kingdom and how we are to live to further God's reign.

SOMETHING ————————————————————————

Something is missing,
something is wrong,
something...

(what vagueness here,
unworthy of any poem
committed to specificity)

So, what is that *some thing*
Original sin may be the cause,
but in what lies the effect?

What's missing? Love!
What's wrong? Lovelessness!

Now that you have the answer,
please don't forget the question.

CROSSING THE TRACKS ————————————————

Last night I crossed the tracks,
left my gloomy mood
and made four phone calls.
The tracks here were not geographic.
My trek was a psychological passage —
from self-absorption to interest in others.

And in that crossing a new freedom came,
relief from imprisoning narcissism.
It is temporary, I know,
but the tracks can be crossed
when grace sets us free.

Consciousness

Why is awareness so difficult,
why such blindness on the journey?
Does the truth hurt that much —
is the noonday light too brilliant for our souls?

It's more than a matter of ignorance.
It's about delusion,
the twisting of facts into fiction,
like a house of distorted mirrors,
the mind playing games with the heart.

O, for the gift of wisdom,
to see what's really there
and not to flinch.
O, for the gift of courage.

Parasites

Guilt is the gap
between the "is" and the "ought."
Shame is the blush upon the cheeks
and eyes downcast.

Guilt looks to the deed (non-deed)
and feels reproach — "That's wrong!"
Shame considers what others think
and feels remorse — more, self-disdain.

Guilt and shame are first cousins,
always in each other's company.
Don't be surprised
if they often sit together at your table.

PAIN

Leaves, as the fire nears,
curl in upon themselves — and are gone.

When suffering circles the human heart
it too folds inward,
drawn there by instinct, for self-protection.
The Spanish proverb got it right
about the world ending at the foot of one's sickbed.

Is there a way out, an alternative response?
Is fire consuming or transforming?
Is suffering destructive or redemptive?
Need the sickbed narrow our world to nothing but self?

When grace is at hand,
a trust in God's redeeming love,
even darkness holds light
and suffering, a hidden joy.
The gift of faith here — sheer grace!

THE JUDGE'S DILEMMA

Daily he sits on the bench.
One after the other, they come before him —
thieves and murderers,
cheats and liars,
drug dealers and con men.
Judgment is passed,
justice seemingly done.

Back in his chambers
the judge ponders, yes, prays.

He, too, is a law-breaker,
not necessarily of the civil law
but surely of the moral, religious code.
He, too, is guilty of harming others,
of neglecting the good to be done,
of fudging on the truth,
failing to affirm, to respect beauty.

Tomorrow he will preside again,
knowing that as the gavel falls
he, too, has a sentence passed on him.

DAMAGED GOODS

Warehouses are full of damaged goods:
a rocking chair scratched up,
a sofa with a tear,
a refrigerator with a caved-in door.
No outlet store will accept these damaged goods.
Yesterday, two individuals, well-known nationally,
identified themselves to me as damaged goods.
Their reputation marred by scandal,
their souls weighed by melancholy.

I have a rocking chair with nicks and scratches,
a sofa threadbare and torn,
a refrigerator that leaks water.
All my friends, like me, are damaged,
flawed, yes, sinful.
None of us is on our way to an outlet store.

OFFENDER _____

Every inmate,
all dressed alike,
wore a nametag.
In greeting them,
I tried to read their names.

The first name stamped in small letters read:
    JOHN.
The surname in slightly larger caps:
    SMITH.

At the top of the tag,
easily visible from some distance,
    OFFENDER.

All inmates alike
in dress and identity.

Another lie
diminishing respect.

LIFE REFERENCE _____

He, the preacher,
spoke of love,
yet said nothing of Mother Teresa
walking the streets of Calcutta.

He spoke of sin,
but made no reference
to King David sleeping with the wife of Uriah.

He spoke of compassion —
of participating in others' joys and sorrows;

again, no connection
with the father — Our Father — of the prodigal son.

Preach to me no more
unless life, real life,
is on your tongue,
and in your words.

I'm Divorced

We were at table,
six third-graders and I, an elder.
I asked about school and family,
sports and Harry Potter.
Animated was our discussion over
tacos and brownies and chocolate milk.
But I left the table sad.
One little third-grade girl,
when asked about her family declared:
"I'm divorced. I have one brother and two step-sisters."
My heart sank.
A nine-year-old "divorcée."
She had taken on the plight of her parents.
Her solidarity bound her up with them.
Her small heart fragmented.
Her voice sad.

I cried on the way home,
for her, for me, for all
of us in broken relationships.

(I never did finish my taco or chocolate milk.)

FULL OF GRACE

(*Archbishop Carlo Maria Martini wrote that "full of grace" means "You have been loved for a very long time."*)

How long have you been loved?
Give me your age and add nine months.
That's how long.
At this very moment — now —
you are being loved,
loved into existence,
loved unto death.

We've all heard the common expression:
"He/she just doesn't get it."

I'm one of those.
When will I get it —
get the insight that I
have been loved for a very long time?
Get the fact that all of us
are full of grace,
beloved and cared for?

Maybe tomorrow?

OUR LADY OF SORROWS

What about joy,
Our Lady of Joys?
But Mary is beneath the cross,
gazing upon her crucified Son,
overwhelmed with grief.

And yet, if deep understanding be had,
there is a joy present
because love is there
between mother and son.
Joy and sorrow dwell in the same house,
on the same day,
in the same hour.
Joy felt because of love,
sorrow in bearing another's pain.

Mary, our Lady of Sorrows and Joys,
ora pro nobis.

The Uglies

Does your heart ever get ugly?
Say, when you are corrected
or you shank a nine iron
or the telemarketer persists after your fourth "no"?

The uglies turn our souls mean,
within a matter of moments,
reversing true conversion
from mellow to mean
instead of from hardness to gentleness.

Yesterday a small comment
led to a large ugly.
It grew huge within seconds
until it soured my voice
and obscured my vision.

It was not a pleasant moment
either for me or those I met.

SHAME

The tears came,
head down
held in both hands.
Suffering.
Pain.
Shame.

We sat in silence.
No anointing words
to soothe the hurt.

We've all been there.
Victims at times;
at others, perpetrators.

It was hard to hold the anguish.
Indeed, I failed
as it fell to the floor.

EASTER EYES

(*"I wish each of us Easter eyes, able to perceive in death, life; in guilt, forgiveness; in separation, unity; in wounds, glory; in the human, God; in God, the human."* — Bishop Klaus Hemmerle)

Easter bonnets and bunnies and eggs,
lilies too,
need a supplement:
Easter eyes.

For to see in death, life,
in guilt, forgiveness,

and in wounds, glory,
is to be a person of the resurrection.

Mary Magdalene had Easter eyes.
She saw (and heard) a gardener and was born anew.
Peter, too,
in looking across a night fire
to perceive in Jesus' eyes forgiveness.
And Thomas?
Doubt vanished when invited to touch those glorious
    wounds.

And you, my soul,
do you have Easter eyes?
Easter tears would seem to say so.

ENVY ———————————————————————

It's not their beauty I envy,
those frogs down at the creek.
Rather, it's the ability
to straddle two worlds.
Comfortable they are on land or sea,
something foreign to bird or bee.

And my two worlds?
Time and Eternity!
When in one, I long for the other;
when in the other, my heart is elsewhere.

Is there some philosophic frog
who, with quiet patience,
might teach me his art
and drain the envy from my heart?

UNDOING

Jesus' gaze undid Peter
and the tears flowed.

Jesus' glance undid Zacchaeus
and a table was set.

Jesus' look of love undid Mary
and her heart was baptized.

It's all about being seen, being loved,
this Christian journey.
It's all about "undoing,"
being set free by Love.

A HOOKED HUMILITY

"Humility with a hook,"
read the marquee outside the church.
I never did hear the sermon,
but here's what the preacher might have said.

"Draw attention to yourself by playing small.
'Ah, shucks,' should be your attitude.
Impress by being unimpressive,
retain egoistical focus by circling the spotlight."

And on and on the preacher goes.
He was proud of his chosen title,
"Humility with a Hook,"
and no one but he
knew his quiet wife wrote it.

CONVERSION _____

On the road,
having fallen to the ground,
Saul turned into Paul.

Under a tree,
finding God's word,
Augustine was set free.

Though seeming sudden,
turning from idols
and clarifying desires
— the process of conversion —
take time, God's time
that we call eternity.

FIFTH STEP _____

Inventories are of different kinds:
the books in the shop,
the tools on the shelf,
the food in the pantry.

And then there is the moral inventory,
a listing of deeds done,
not done,
throughout the course of one's entire life.

What rawness here.
What brutal honesty.
What freedom and peace.

Yes, and what joy.

JUDGMENT

Some receive judgment now —
their deeds exposed to a judge and jury
and a sentence declared.

Others, their crimes more internal,
remain on the street —
their deeds hidden from public gaze.

Regardless, judgment will come —
it cannot be eternally deferred.
But when it does come,
the divine sentence
will be laden with mercy.

OUT OF PLACE

Where is your place?
Is it the chemistry lab,
the emergency room,
the cloister or the hearth,
perhaps the farm or the factory?
Wherever it is, find it;
wherever it is not, leave it.

To be out of place
leads to being out of sorts
that leads to being nowhere.

Place is about space.
More, it is about finding the room
that is your true home.

COMMUNION _____

Wednesday I was one with history
spending two and a half hours in the Civil War
with all its brutality and glory.

Thursday I was one with nature
trimming evergreens for five hours at the farm
in the quietness, coldness of a winter day.

Now I am one with myself
reflecting for twenty minutes on communion,
union, unity with history and nature and self.

Why then do I feel alienated?

UNSETTLED _____

Would that things were settled:
the garden weedless,
correspondence all answered,
the check book balanced,
relationships harmonious, peaceful.

Such is not the case —
life itself is unsettling
with its weeds and spats,
its laundry always there,
its duties demanding care.

Being unsettled is a gift,
a blessing in disguise.
It keeps us on the move,
however turtle-like,
drawing us to a final harvest.

DISCREET FESTIVITY

(*"But this festivity must also remain discreet, lest it insult the immense pain of millions of women and men who throughout the world continue to live in despair."* — Louis-Marie Chauvet)

No wet-blanket here,
just high sensitivity for those who suffer
while we enjoy —
enjoy the wine at Cana,
enjoy the sudden gift of friendship.
enjoy the surgery restoring health.

Be discreet in these festivities.
Yes, dance and sing and be merry
but, before falling asleep,
remember unto the Lord all those,
millions upon millions,
who have no wine or friends,
who live near the edge of despair.

THE SCREWTAPE LETTERS

(*On rereading C. S. Lewis's* The Screwtape Letters)

It's a federal offense —
opening and reading others' mail.
But correspondence from a devil,
ah, all is fair in love and hell.

I've read and reread these letters
now going on twenty years.
Each time I am convicted —

of game playing,
of tedious narcissism,
of subtle arrogance,
of pernicious pride.

I tried to burn these epistles
but they were already on fire
and yet not consumed.

No burning bush here
but evil incarnate.

SNIT _____

To get bit by a snit
means someone's going to be hit
with a stare,
a menacing glare,
as hostility fills the air.

It happened last evening.
Amid smiles and laughter,
a snit bit my soul.
The black clouds descended,
an ugly mood moved in,
and though laughter still rang,
now my soul knew emotional pain.

This state of agitation has a simple cause —
I was not having my way.
This is a good walk spoiled
and a cheerful evening soiled.

KIND WORDS

(Al Capone: "You get more done with a kind word and a gun than with a kind word alone.")

Does God tote a gun?
One would think not,
this God who speaks tenderly to his people,
who is called Love,
who is known as Mercy.

Yet David felt the bullets of accusation,
via Nathan, God's prophet.
Even Peter's heart was riddled with buckshot
as Jesus glanced across the evening fire of betrayal.
And were not the nails rifled through Jesus' hands and
　　feet
somehow a part of a divine design?

I sit here in (apparent) safety
pondering whether or not God has an arsenal
beside his lexicon of kind words.

KING LEAR POEM — I

("Wisdom and goodness to the vile seem vile."
IV, ii, l. 38)

We all wear glasses.
Everything seen is filtered
by the moods of the heart,
our individual intellectual platform,
the cultural garden we live in.

Hitler saw the Jewish people.
In his blindness and hatred
he condemned them to death.

Mother Teresa saw the poor of Calcutta.
In her wisdom and hope
she gave them new life.

Whatever is received is received
according to the mode and moods of the receiver.

To the vile, all things are vile;
to the virtuous, grace is everywhere.

KING LEAR POEM — II

(*"As flies to wanton boys are we to th' gods;
They kill us for their sport."* IV, i, ll. 35–36)

Cruelty is not foreign to the human heart.
Boys kill flies — for the fun of it —
as men go on safari for the fun of it.
From whence this arbitrary violence?
From the gods in whose image we are made?

We seek the cause for our affliction;
we seek to assign responsibility for our misfortune.
Why not glance at wanton boys
and transpose their deeds to supernatural powers.

Why not look within
and there find our own sin.

ADDICTION _____

What is it?
A moral lapse?
A disease?
Or, something else?

The "it" is addiction —
be it to alcohol,
tobacco, cybersex
or Orville Redenbacher's gourmet popping corn.

The experts say it's a disease
while others name it sin.
Whatever,
freedom is diminished if not absent
and the addict is trapped, severely impaired.

Last night an addict spoke,
told his story of enslavement to booze
and, by so doing, set us free.

THE PLAY _____

While reading "Hamlet,"
while reading of madness and methods,
of murder and misguided love,
of revenge and deception,
I asked:
"Is this reality?"

I put the Bard down,
walked out into daylight,
and met Polonius at a luncheon meeting,

Ophelia down at the mall, buying flowers,
Horatio at Barnes and Noble,
and young Hamlet at Fleet Farm.

Is life a play,
are dramas life?

The Bard was right once again:
the whole world is a stage
and we, actors all.

CHANGE

Is change possible,
deep, abiding change, that is?
My friends and I read a book,
a story of many people —
no one changed!
The alcoholic still drank,
the grouch only got grouchier,
the domineering mistress sought more control.

The bottom line:
we are what we are what we are.

On my desk is an acorn.
Outside my window I saw a caterpillar.
In my mind's eye
an oak tree and butterfly appeared.

Yes, we are what we are
but what we can be still abides.

THE GAP

Between the "is" and the "ought"
there is a gap.
Wide for some,
narrower for others.
But it is there,
never to be totally closed here on earth.

That gap is the land of guilt.
What should be, isn't;
what is, should be more.

The gap, I mean, between
the real and the ideal,
the actual and the potential,
yes, the sinner and the saint.

Thus, we all are struggling pilgrims,
all dwelling in-between
what we are and are called to be.

> Be patient, therefore.
> Have compassion.
> Trust in a merciful God.

FEAR

Make a list of them,
those fears that fill your heart
and disturb your nights and days.
The fear of public opinion —
     what others might say;

the fear of time and eternity —
    creatures of things transitory;
the fear of love —
    its unrelenting demands;
the fear of existence —
    the enigma, the mystery of being.

"Laugh, creature, and be not afraid,"
the advice of one wisdom figure.
What a grace!
What great courage!
What faith!

THE CROSS

(*On reading E. Herman's* The Finding of the Cross)

No less a mystery — the cross —
after pondering this text.
Suffering and I lack compatibility.
Penance and penitence too a foreign language.
So much have I to learn
about the way of the cross.
When will I learn not to run from Calvary?

Maybe we never find the cross —
this extravagant self-giving love of Jesus —
maybe it is the cross that finds us.

THE LION'S SHARE ────────────────────

I always get the lamb's share,
the smallest chocolate chip cookie,
minimal wage,
hand-me down jackets,
beaten up baseballs.

I always get the lamb's share,
I'm six years old.
My brother? He gets the lion's share.
        He's nine.

Life isn't fair.

DELIVERANCE ────────────────────

To be set free!

The beaver from the trap,
the alcoholic from drink,
the addict from cocaine,
the sinner from death.

And the Deliverer?

God's grace,
holy asceticism.

What spaciousness,
what peace,
what joy.

A THIRD TESTAMENT _____

(*On reading Malcolm Muggeridge's* A Third Testament)

the first testament — the old one —
tells of life's struggles and tempests.
we hear of David and Job,
Isaiah and Saul, Eve and Ruth.
they all bore a unique witness
to God's grace in their life.

the second testament — the new one —
tells of struggling pilgrims as well.
there's John the Baptist and the rich young man,
Saul/Paul and the turbulent Peter,
Martha and her master, Jesus.
they all witnessed, bore testimony
to the mystery of God's love.

now a third testament — modern? post-modern? —
tales of flawed, holy sinners
striving toward the Light of Reality.
Augustine and Pascal,
Blake and Kierkegaard,
Dostoevsky, Tolstoy, and Bonhoeffer.
no women here such as
Dorothy Day and Therese,
Sojourner Truth and Clare,
Anne Frank, Julian of Norwich, and Flannery
      O'Connor.
Testifiers all of them are
to God's light and love and life.

Notes

Introduction

1. Dogmatic Constitution on the Church, *Lumen Gentium*, no. 1 (promulgated by Pope Paul VI, November 21, 1964).

1: The Mystery of God's Mercy

1. *Selected Poetry of Jessica Powers*, ed. Regina Siegfried, A.S.C., and Robert F. Morneau (Kansas City: Sheed & Ward, 1989), 21.

2. Pope John Paul II, *Dives in Misericordia*, November 1980.

3. Sister Anne Higgins, D.C., unpublished poem; used with the permission of the author.

2: The Mystery of the Human Person

1. James J. Bacik, *Spirituality in Action* (Kansas City, Mo.: Sheed & Ward, 1997), 46–47.

2. William James, *The Varieties of Religious Experience: A Study of Human Nature* (New York: Modern Library, 1936), 349.

3. Dietrich von Hildebrand, *Transformation in Christ: On the Christian Attitude* (San Francisco: Ignatius Press, 2001), 75.

4. John Macquarrie, *Mary for All Christians* (Grand Rapids, Mich.: William B. Eerdmans, 1990), 108.

5. Joseph Conrad, *Lord Jim* (New York: International Collectors Library, 1899, 1920), 131.

6. Timothy Radcliffe, O.P., *Sing a New Song: The Christian Vocation* (Springfield, Ill.: Templegate Publishers, 1999), 223.

7. Caryll Houselander, *The Reed of God* (Allen, Tex.: Christian Classics, 1944), 96.

3: The Context for Reconciliation

1. C. S. Lewis, *Surprised by Joy: The Shape of My Early Years* (New York: Harcourt Brace Jovanovich, 1955), 229.

2. Mother Teresa of Calcutta, *A Gift for God: Prayers and Meditations* (New York: HarperCollins, 1975), 29.

3. Timothy Radcliffe O.P., *Sing a New Song: The Christian Vocation* (Springfield, Ill.: Templegate Publishers, 1999), 144.

4. Iain Pears, *The Dream of Scipio* (New York: Riverhead Books, 2002), 52.

5. *The Roman Pontifical* (International Committee on English in the Liturgy, Inc., 1978), 77.

6. Raïssa Maritain, *We Have Been Friends Together* (New York: Longmans, Green, 1942), 31.

7. Evelyn Underhill, *The House of the Soul*; *Concerning the Inner Life* (Minneapolis: Seabury Press, 1984), p. 141 in *Concerning the Inner Life*.

8. Romano Guardini, *The Lord* (Chicago: Henry Regnery, 1954), 434.

9. C. S. Lewis, *Mere Christianity* (San Francisco: HarperSanFrancisco, 2001), 164.

10. Fyodor Dostoevsky, *The Brothers Karamazov* (New York: International Collectors Library, 1960), 291.

11. Aelred Squire, *Asking the Fathers* (Westminster, Md.: Christian Classics, 1993), 10.

4: *The Mystery of Sin*

1. Robert F. Morneau, *Poems Thrown into the Wind* (De Pere, Wisc.: Paisa Publishing Company, 2003), 58.

2. George Herbert, *The Country Parson, The Temple* (New York: Paulist Press, 1981), 184.

3. Brigid E. Herman, *Creative Prayer* (Brewster, Mass.: Paraclete Press, 1998), 9–10.

4. *The Collected Works of St. John of the Cross*, trans. Kieran Kavanaugh, O.C.D., and Otilio Rodriguez, O.C.D. (Washington, D.C.: Institute of Carmelite Studies, 1973), 244–45.

5. Georges Bernanos, *The Diary of a Country Priest*, trans. Pamela Morris (New York: Doubleday, 1954), 98.

6. Ralph Waldo Emerson, "New England Reformers," *The Selected Writings of Ralph Waldo Emerson*, ed. with a biographical introduction by Brooks Atkinson (New York: Random House, 1940), 218.

7. Thomas Merton, *The Seven Storey Mountain* (New York: Harcourt, Brace, 1948), 294–95.

8. *Raïssa's Journal*, presented by Jacques Maritain (Albany, N.Y.: Magi Books, 1963), 115.

5: *Principles of Reconciliation*

1. Michael Downey, "Consenting to Kenosis: Mission to Secularity," in Ronald Rolheiser, *Secularity and the Gospel: Being Missionaries to Our Children* (New York: Crossroad, 2006), 132–33.

2. Robert Schreiter, C.PP.S., "Pathways to New Evangelization in the First World," in ibid., 114–15.

3. Abraham Heschel, *Man's Quest for God* (New York: Charles Scribner's Sons, 1954), 102.

4. John Macquarrie, *Principles of Christian Theology,* 2nd ed. (New York: Charles Scribner's Sons, 1977), 268.

5. Rolheiser, *Secularity and the Gospel,* 77.

6. *An Anthology of the Love of God* from the writings of Evelyn Underhill, ed. Lumsden Barkway and Lucy Menzies (London: Mowbray, 1976), 186.

7. William Shakespeare's *Hamlet,* Act III, sc. iii, ll. 51–55.

8. C. S. Lewis, *Mere Christianity* (New York: Macmillan, 1974), 149.

9. Michael Mayne, *Pray, Love, Remember* (London: Darton, Longman and Todd, 1998), 46.

10. Dana Greene, *Evelyn Underhill: Artist of the Infinite Life* (New York: Crossroad, 1990), 150.

11. Gregory Baum, *Man Becoming* (New York: Herder and Herder, 1970), 134.

12. Thomas R. Kelly, *A Testament of Devotion* (New York: Harper-Collins Publishers, 1992), 67.

13. Yves Congar, *I Believe in the Holy Spirit,* vol. 3, trans. David Smith (New York: Crossroad, 1983), 149.

14. Hans Urs von Balthasar, *Prayer,* trans. A. V. Littledale (New York: Sheed & Ward, 1961), 235.

15. *The Letters of Caryll Houselander: Her Spiritual Legacy,* ed. Maisie Ward (New York: Sheed and Ward, 1965), 115.

16. John Shea, *Stories of God: An Unauthorized Biography* (Chicago: Thomas More Association, 1978), 152.

17. Judith Viorst, *Necessary Losses* (New York: Simon & Schuster, 1986), 139.

18. William Lynch, *Images of Hope* (Notre Dame, Ind.: University of Notre Dame Press, 1965), 206.

19. Dante Alighieri, *The Divine Comedy,* "Inferno," Canto XIII, trans. Lawrence Grant White (New York: Pantheon Books, 1948).

20. Thomas Merton, *The Seven Storey Mountain* (New York: Harcourt, Brace, 1948), 33.

21. François Roustang, S.J., *Growth in the Spirit,* trans. Kathleen Pond (New York: Sheed and Ward, 1963), 51–52.

22. Paul Tillich, *The Shaking of the Foundations* (New York: Charles Scribner's Sons, 1948), 154–55.

23. Brigid E. Herman, *Creative Prayer* (Brewster, Mass.: Paraclete Press, 1998), 157.

24. Jim Wallis, *The Call to Conversion* (San Francisco: Harper & Row Publishers, 1981), 47.

25. Mohandas K. Gandhi, *Autobiography: The Story of My Experiments with Truth,* trans. Mahadev Desai (New York: Dover Publications, 1948), 24.

26. Dietrich Bonhoeffer, *Life Together* (New York: Harper & Row, 1954), 112.

27. Howard Bleichner, *View from the Altar: Reflections on the Changing Catholic Priesthood* (New York: Crossroad, 2004), 86.

28. John Irving, *A Prayer for Owen Meany* (New York: Ballantine Books, 1989), 617.

29. Quote from Karl Rahner; source unknown.

30. Greene, *Evelyn Underhill,* 20.

31. Flannery O'Connor, *Mystery and Manners,* selected and edited by Sally and Robert Fitzgerald (New York: Farrar, Straus & Giroux, 1962), 118.

32. Ladislaus Boros, *Hidden God,* trans. Erika Young (New York: Seabury Press, 1971), 84.

33. Robert D. Lupton, *Theirs Is the Kingdom* (San Francisco: Harper & Row, 1989), 13.

6: Sacrament of Reconciliation

1. Cited in Thomas C. Fox, *Pentecost in Asia: A New Way of Being Church* (Maryknoll, N.Y.: Orbis Books, 2002), 9.

2. Anne Morrow Lindbergh, *Gift from the Sea* (New York: Random House, Vintage Books Edition, 1965), 17.

3. Brigid E. Herman, *Creative Prayer* (Brewster, Mass.: Paraclete Press, 1998), 23.

4. Cited in Kay Redfield Jamison, *An Unquiet Mind: A Memoir of Moods and Madness* (New York: Vintage Books, 1995), 146.

5. *Francis de Sales, Jane de Chantal: Letters of Spiritual Direction,* trans. Peronne Marie Thibert, V.H.M (New York: Paulist Press, 1988), 159.

6. *Selected Poetry of Jessica Powers,* ed. Regina Siegfried, A.S.C., and Robert F. Morneau (Kansas City, Mo.: Sheed & Ward, 1989), 197.

7: Questions and Answers

1. William Shakespeare's *Romeo and Juliet,* Act I, sc. 1, ll. 152–53.

2. C. S. Lewis, *The Screwtape Letters* (New York: Macmillan, 1961), 132.

3. Karl Rahner, *The Need and Blessing of Prayer* (Collegeville, Minn.: Liturgical Press, 1997), 93.

4. Timothy Radcliffe O.P., *What Is the Point of Being a Christian?* (New York: Burns & Oates, 2005), 149.

"Truly a spirituality for the 21st century!"
— *Dolores Leckey*

Catholic Spirituality for Adults

General Editor
Michael Leach

Forthcoming volumes include:

- *Holiness* by William O'Malley
- *Diversity of Vocations* by Marie Dennis
- *Charity* by Virgil Elizondo
- *Listening to God's Word* by Alice Camille
- *Community* by Adela Gonzalez
- *Incarnation* by John Shea
- And many others.

To learn more about forthcoming titles in the series, go to *orbisbooks.com*.

To learn more about resources for total parish catechesis, including children's materials that cover the same topics as *Catholic Spirituality for Adults,* please visit rclbenziger.com.

Please support your local bookstore.

Thank you for reading *Reconciliation* by Robert Morneau. We hope you found it beneficial.